THE PIXY BOOK

FRANCIS COCKERTON

TOR MARK PRESS · PENRYN

The folk tales in this book were collected in Devon or in East Cornwall in Victorian times. They are related here mainly in the words of the collectors, but edited to avoid archaic words and phrases.

The main sources are:

Mrs Bray (1790-1883), wife of the vicar of Tavistock, writing in the 1830s to impress her friend the Poet Laureate Southey;

William Crossing (1847-1928), who devoted much of his life to the study of Dartmoor and wrote what is still a best-selling guide to walking on the moor;

Jonathan Couch (1789-1870), a scientist who wrote a monumental four volume account of the fishes of the British Isles. and in the 1850s a *History of Polperro.*

The Tor Mark series

Folklore

Classic Cornish ghost stories
Classic Devon ghost stories
Classic West Country ghost stories
Cornish fairies
Cornish folklore
Cornish legends
Customs and superstitions in Cornish folklore
Demons, ghosts and spectres in Cornish folklore
Devonshire customs and superstitions
Devonshire legends
The pixy book

Other titles

Charlestown
China clay
Classic Cornish anecdotes
Cornish fishing industry
Cornish mining – at surface
Cornish mining – underground
Cornish mining industry
Cornish recipes
Cornish saints
Cornwall in camera
Cornwall's early lifeboats
Cornwall's engine houses
Cornwall's railways
Devonshire jokes and stories
Do you know Cornwall?
Exploring Cornwall with your car
Harry Carter – Cornish smuggler
Houses, castles and gardens in Cornwall
Introducing Cornwall
King Arthur – man or myth?
Lost ports of Cornwall
Old Cornwall – in pictures
The pasty book
Shipwrecks around Land's End
Shipwrecks around the Lizard
Shipwrecks around Mounts Bay
Shipwrecks - Falmouth to Looe
South-east Cornwall
The story of Cornwall
The story of the Cornish language
The story of St Ives
The story of Truro Cathedral
Tales of the Cornish fishermen
Tales of the Cornish miners
Tales of the Cornish smugglers
Tales of the Cornish wreckers

First published 1996 by Tor Mark Press,
Islington Wharf, Penryn, Cornwall TR10 8AT

ISBN 0-85025-349-7
The cover illustration is by Beryl Sanders
Printed in Cornwall, UK, by Cornwall Litho, Redruth

What's the difference between a pixy and a fairy?

A Devonshire writer's nurse told him that a fairy wears clothes while a pixy goes naked, but this is simply untrue. Pixies in traditional stories are generally dressed in green, with red hoods, and there is no record of any pixy naturists!

The truth is a little confused, because even within the West Country, the word 'pixy' – or more commonly 'pisky' or 'pisgy' – means different things in different places.

In Devon and eastern Cornwall all the 'little people' came to be known collectively as pixies. In the far west of Cornwall, on the other hand, the old distinctions between different races of fairy survived. Around Land's End in Victorian times, the word 'Pisky' was almost always used in the singular, rather like the name of a god – which quite possibly he once was.

Pisky in this sense was the spirit which Shakespeare in *Midsummer Night's Dream* called Puck, the spirit

> That frights the maidens of the villagery...
> And bootless makes the breathless housewife churn,
> And sometime makes the drink to bear no barm,
> Misleads night wanderers, laughing at their harm?
> Those that Hobgoblin call you and sweet Puck,
> You do their work and they shall have good luck.

The sheer unpredictability and contrariness of life, which with our superior scientific knowledge we now know to be governed by Murphy's Law, was attributed by our ancestors to the activities of Pisgy, or Puck, or Robin Goodfellow, or as the ancient Greeks knew him, the god Pan, inspirer of panic.

In the far west there was a rich variety of fairy races – 'the little people', brownies, spriggans and knockers, as well as Pisky. You will find traditional stories of these creatures in *Cornish Fairies* by Robert Hunt in this series.

In this book, however, our pixies are the kinds found in north and east Cornwall and on Dartmoor. Travellers in these tales may well be 'pisky-led' by Puck, without seeing him, but when they meet pixies all the distinctions between different kinds of creatures have been lost.

How did people account for fairies?

Folklorists think that the pixies may be the hazy memory of an older religion or religions. Perhaps they were originally the 'spirits' of trees and brooks, like the nymphs of Greek and Roman mythology. Certainly the stories of monks trying to eliminate pixies suggest some religious rivalry.

But the people who told these stories usually explained the pixies as the souls of unbaptised children, or of pre-Christian ancestors, who would not be allowed into heaven, or of Druids who had perversely refused to be converted.

Did people really believe in the pixies?

Before the eighteenth century most country people all over Britain probably believed in the little people. These beliefs died out slowly, and the west of England, like the Highlands of Scotland, clung hardest to them. By the time writers began to collect these stories, which till then had been told only by travelling story-tellers and by the old folk around the fireside, perhaps some of them were told with a twinkle in the eye. Yet they were believed or part-believed by their audiences.

Some pixy stories are told in a way which suggests drunkenness, practical joking, or even crime: smugglers would spread stories of pixies, ghosts and the devil to deter people from walking at night and seeing more than they should, or to explain sudden wealth or pack-horses mysteriously exhausted at dawn.

Yet many people really did sometimes turn their clothes inside out, or put a prayer book under their pillow, as a protective measure, and it was reported in 1879 that a Dartmoor farmer, whose cattle were dying of an infection, sacrificed a sheep to the pixies he thought were causing it, which is certainly a measure of his belief. Mothers desperate over a child with an illness or disfigurement sometimes convinced themselves that they had a changeling, rather than face up to the truth. And to be lost on a boggy moor in fog is (I can vouch for it) a terrifying experience likely to make the imagination run riot. The pixies were a way of making sense of stressful events.

Today, many people apparently believe in guardian angels, and many others that they have been abducted into alien spacecraft and returned among us. We have no cause to laugh at our ancestors' credulity!

As education spread, country people became aware that if they showed they believed in fairies, they might be laughed at behind their backs, so they began to hide their belief. This makes it hard to know how recently belief continued, but even today there are people – admittedly, mainly in-comers! – who admit to having seen pixies.

Pixy lore in Polperro – Jonathan Couch, writing about 1850

The belief in the little folk is far from dead among us, although the people of this generation are less certain of it than their forefathers, and are aware that piskies are now fair objects of ridicule, whatever they may formerly have been. One old woman in particular, to whose recital of some of the following tales I have listened in mute attention, was a firm believer in them; and I well remember her pettish reply when a young friend of mine ventured to hint a doubt: 'What! not believe in mun, when my poor mother hath been pinched black and blue by mun!' The argument was conclusive to us, for we could not then see its fallacy, though we have since learned that the poor soul in question had not the kindest of husbands.

The creed has received so many additions and modifications that it is impossible to make any arrangement of our Polperro fairies into classes. 'The elves of the hills, brooks, standing lakes, and groves' are all now confounded under the generic name pisky. Our piskies are little beings standing midway between the purely spiritual and the material, suffering a few, at least, of the ills incident to humanity. They have the power of making themselves seen, heard or felt. They interest themselves in man's affairs; now doing him a good turn, then suddenly taking offence at a trifle, and leading him into all manner of mischief. The clumsy gratitude of the farmer is taken as an insult, and the capricious sprites mislead him on the first opportunity, and laugh heartily at his misadventures. They are great enemies of slovenliness and encouragers of good husbandry. When not singing or dancing, their chief nightly amusement is in riding the colts, and plaiting the manes, or tangling them with the seed vessels of the burdock. Of a particular field in this neighbourhood it is reported that the farmer never puts his horses in it but he finds them in the morning in a state of great terror, panting and covered with foam.

Their form of government is monarchical, as frequent mention is made of the 'King of the piskies'. We have a few stories of pisky changelings, the only proof of whose parentage is that 'they didn't goodey' (thrive). It would seem that fairy children of some age are entrusted to mortal care for a time, and again recalled to pisky-land. People are occasionally kidnapped by the little folk; hence an old nursery rhyme says;

See saw, Margery Daw
Sold her bed and lay upon straw;
She sold her straw and lay upon hay,
Piskies came and carr'd her away.

A disposition to laughter is a striking trait in their character, and a person who laughs heartily and unrestrainedly is said to 'laugh like a pisky'. I have been able to gather little about the personality of these beings. My old friend, before mentioned, described them as about a span [say nine inches] long, clad in green and wearing straw hats or little red caps on their heads. Two only are known by name and I have heard them addressed in the following rhyme:

Jack o'the lantern! Joan the wad,
Who tickled the maid and made her mad;
Light me home, the weather's bad.

Tavistock pixies – Mrs Bray, writing in the 1830s

I have not yet said much about our bogs on the moor, which from some luckless horse or other being now and then lost in them, have obtained as their popular name that of the 'Dartmoor stables'. These bogs in old times must have been exceedingly dangerous; even now that we have a road through the moor which displays all the happy results of Mr McAdam's genius, yet nevertheless if a mist suddenly comes on, the stranger feels no small concern for his own safety.

Mr Bray assures me that when he used, in early life, to follow up with enthusiasm his researches on the moor, not heeding the weather, he has frequently been suddenly surprised and enveloped in such a dense mist that he literally could scarcely see the ears of the animal on which he rode. Once or twice he was in some peril by getting on boggy ground, when his horse, more terrified than himself, would shake and tremble in every joint, and become covered in foam from the extreme agony of fear.

If such adventures have now and then happened even in these days, how far more frequently must they have occurred when there was no regular road across the moor! How often a traveller, if he escaped with his life, must have wandered about for hours in such a wilderness before he could fall into any known or beaten track, to lead him from his perils towards the ancient town of Tavistock, or the villages with which it is surrounded!

I mention this because I think there cannot be a doubt that similar distresses gave rise to the popular belief still existing, not only on the moor but throughout all this neighbourhood, that whenever a person loses his way, he is neither more nor less than 'pixy-led'.

The good dames in this part of the world are very particular in sweeping their houses before going to bed, and they frequently place a basin of water by the chimney nook, to be helpful to the pixies, who are great lovers of water; and sometimes the pixies pay back the good deed by dropping a piece of money in the basin. A young woman of our town, who declared she had received the reward of sixpence for a like service, told the circumstance to her gossips; but no sixpence ever came again, and it was generally believed that the pixies had taken offence by her chattering, as they don't like to have their deeds, good or evil, talked over by mortal tongues.

Many a pixy is sent out on works of mischief, to deceive the old nurses and to steal away young children, or to do them harm. Many also, bent on mischief, are sent forth to lead poor travellers astray, to deceive them with those false lights called Will-o'the-wisp, or to guide them in a fine dance in trudging home through woods and waters, through bogs and quagmires and every peril.

Others, who content themselves with a practical joke, and who love frolic more than mischief, will merely make sport by blowing out the candles on a sudden, or kissing the maids 'with a smack', so that they shriek out 'who's this?' – till their grandmothers come and lecture them for allowing unseemly freedoms with young men.

Some are sent out to frolic or make noises in wells; and the more gentle and kindly of the race will spin flax and help their favourite damsels to do their work. I have heard a story about an old woman in this town who suspected she received assistance of this nature, and one evening coming suddenly into the room, she spied a ragged little creature who jumped out at the door. She thought she would try still further to win the services of her elfin friend, and so bought some smart new clothes, as big as those made for a doll. These pretty things she placed by the side of her wheel; the pixy returned and put them on; when, clapping her tiny hands in joy, she was hear to exclaim these lines:

> Pixy fine, pixy gay,
> Pixy now will run away.

And off she went, but the ungrateful little creature never spun for the old woman after.

The wicked and thievish elves, who are all said to be squint-eyed, are despatched on the dreadful errand of changing children in the cradle. In such cases (so say our gossips in Devon) the pixies behave to the stolen child just as the mortal mother may happen to behave towards the changeling dropped in its stead. I have been assured that mothers who credit these idle tales pin their children to their sides in order to secure them; though even this precaution has proved useless, so cunning are the elves. I heard a story not long ago about a woman who lived and died in this town and who most solemnly declared that her mother had a child that was changed by the pixies whilst she, good dame, was busied in hanging out some linen to dry in her garden. She almost broke her heart on discovering the cheat, but took the greatest care of the changeling; which so pleased the pixy mother, that some time later she returned the stolen child, who was ever after very lucky.

It is reported that in days of old, as well as in the present time, the wild waste of Dartmoor was much haunted by spirits and pixies in every direction; and these frequently left their own lands to exercise their mischievous tricks and gambols even in the town of Tavistock itself – despite the fact that it was then guarded by its stately abbey, well stocked with monks, who made war on the pixy race 'with bell, book and candle' at every opportunity. And it is also alleged that the devil (who if not absolutely the father, is assuredly the ally of all mischief) gave the pixies his powerful aid in all manner of delusion. Sometimes he would carry his audacity so far as to enter the venerable abbey grounds, always, however, carefully avoiding the holy water – a thing which would transform him from whatever disguise he was using into his own true shape and person. But the good people here state that these days the clergy are more learned than formerly, and the burial service so much enlarged compared to what it was in earlier days, that the spirits are more closely controlled, and the pixies held tolerably fast, and conjured away to their own domains.

Pixies are said to congregate together, even by their thousands, in some of those wild and desolate places where there is no church. In a field near Down-house, there is a pit which the pixies, not very long ago, appropriated for their ball room. There, in the depths of the night, the owl, who probably stood as sentry for the company, would hoot between whiles; and sounds such as never came from mortal voice or touch would float in the air, whilst the elves would whirl in giddy round.

Whitchurch Down is said to be very famous for the peril of there being pixy-led; for there many an honest yeoman and stout farmer, especially if he should happen to take a cup too much, is very apt to lose his way; and whenever he does so he will declare, and offer to take his Bible oath upon it, 'That as sure as ever he's alive to tell it, whilst his head was running round like a mill-wheel, he heard with his own ears they bits of pisgies, a-laughing and a-tacking their hands, all to see he led astray and never able to find the right road, though he'd travelled it scores of times previous, by night or by day, as a body might tell.' And many good old folks relate the same thing, and how pisgies delight to lead the aged a-wandering about after dark.

But as most evils set men's wits to work to find out a remedy for them, even so we in this part of the world have worked out our remedies against such tiresome tricks. For whoever finds himself pixy-led, has nothing more to do than to turn jacket, petticoat, pocket or apron inside out, and a pixy, who hates the sight of impropriety in dress, cannot stand this; and off the imp goes, as if he'd been sent packing with a flea in his ear.

Now this turning of jackets, petticoats, etc, being found so good as a remedy, was then tried as a preventive; and as some good mother may may now and then be prevailed with to give her darling Doctor Such-a-one's panacea to keep off a disease before it makes an appearance, even so do our good old townsfolk practise this turning inside-out ere they venture on a walk after sundown near any suspected place, as a certain preventive against being led astray by a pixy.

John Taprail and the piskies

John Taprail, long since dead, moored his boat one evening beside a barge of much larger size, in which his neighbour, John Rundle, traded between Polperro and Plymouth. The wind, though gusty, was not sufficient to be worrying, so he went to bed and slept soundly. In the middle of the night he was awoken by a voice outside, bidding him to get up, and 'shift his rope over Rundle's barge,' as his own boat was in danger. Now as all Taprail's capital was in his boat and gear, we may be sure that he was not long in putting on his sea clothes and going to its rescue. To his great chagrin he found that a joke had been played upon him, for the boat and barge were both riding quietly at their ropes. On his way back again, when within a few yards of his home, he observed a crowd of little people crowded under the shelter of a boat that was lying high and dry upon the beach. They were sitting in a semi-circle holding their hats towards one of the number, who was engaged in distributing a heap of money, pitching a gold piece into each hat in succession.

Now John had a covetous heart, and the sight of so much cash made him forget the respect due to an assembly of piskies, and that they were not slow to punish any intrusion on their privacy; so he crept slyly towards them, hidden by the boat, and reaching round, managed to introduce his hat without exciting any notice. When the heap was getting low, and Taprail was awakening to the dangers of detection, he craftily withdrew his hat and made off with the prize. He had got a fair start before the trick was discovered, but the defrauded piskies were soon on his heels, and he barely managed to reach his house and to close the doors upon his pursuers. So narrow indeed was his escape that he left the tails of his sea-coat in their hands.

The midwife and the ointment

Once upon a time there was, in Tavistock, a Dame Somebody. I do not know her name, and as she was a real person, I have no right to give a fictitious one. All I can say is that she was old, and nothing worse for that, for age is, or ought to be, held in honour as the source of wisdom and experience. Now this good old woman had passed her days in the useful capacity of a nurse; and as she approached the time of going out of the world herself, she made herself useful by helping others into it. She was in fact a midwife.

One night, about twelve o'clock, Dame Somebody had just got comfortably into bed when rap, rap, rap, came on her cottage door, with such bold, loud and continued noise that there was a sound of authority in every single knock. Startled and alarmed by the call, she arose from her bed and soon learned that the summons was a hasty one to a patient who needed her help. She opened her door and saw the visitor. He was a strange, squint-eyed, ugly, little old fellow, who had a look, as she said, very like a certain dark and unholy personage who ought not to be called by his proper name. The messenger's face did not make her any more enthusiastic for late night nursing, but she could not or dared not resist the command to follow him straightaway, and attend upon 'his wife'.

'Thy wife,' thought the good dame. 'Heaven forgive me, but as sure as I live I be going to the birth of a little divel.'

A large coal-black horse, with eyes like balls of fire, stood at the door. The ill-looking fellow whisked her up without more ado onto a high pillion, seated himself before her, and away went horse and riders, as if sailing through the air rather than trotting on the ground. How Dame Somebody got to the place of her destination she could not tell; they went so fast she shut her eyes. But it was a great relief when she found herself set down at the door of a neat cottage, saw a couple of tidy children, and remarked her patient to be a decent-looking woman who had everything properly organized for the time and occasion.

A fine bouncing babe soon made its appearance, which seemed very bold on its entry into life, for it gave the good dame a box on the ear, when with the coaxing and cajolery of all the good old midwives, she declared the 'sweet little thing is very like its father.' The mother said nothing to this, but gave the nurse a certain ointment with directions that she should 'strike the child's eye with it.' Now you must know that this word strike in our Devonshire vocabulary does not mean to hit, but rather to rub, smooth, or touch gently. The nurse performed her task, though she thought it an odd one; she wondered what it could be for; and thought that, as no doubt it was a good thing, she might just as well try it upon her own eyes as well as on those of the baby; so she made free to strike one of them by way of trial; when, O ye powers of fairyland! what a change was there!

The neat but homely cottage, and all who were in it, seemed all of a sudden to undergo a mighty transformation; some for the better, some for the worse. The new-made mother appeared as a beautiful lady attired in white; the babe was seen wrapped in swaddling clothes of a silvery gauze. It looked much prettier than before, but still maintained the elfish cast of the eye, like his father; whilst two or three children more had undergone a horrid change. For there sat on either side of the bed a couple of little flat-nosed imps, who with many a grimace and grin, were playing around, scratching their own heads, or pulling the fairy lady's ears with their long and hairy paws.

The nurse, seeing all this and fearing she knew not what in this house of enchantment, got away as fast as she could. She didn't say one word about striking her own eye with the magic ointment, or what she had seen in consequence of doing so. The sour old fellow once more handed her up on the coal-black horse, and sent her home 'in a whip-sissa'. (Now, what a whip-sissa means is more than I can tell, but certain it is that the old woman came home much faster than she went.)

On the next market day, when she sallied forth to sell her eggs, who should she see but the same wicked-looking old fellow, busied like a rogue in pilfering all sorts of things from stall to stall.

'Oh ho!' thought the dame, 'have I caught you, you old thief? But I'll let you see I could set master mayor and the two town constables on your back, if I choose to be telling.' So up to him she went, with that bold, free sort of air, which persons who have learned secrets they ought not to know are apt to assume. She asked casually after his wife and child, and hoped both were as well as could be expected.

'What!' exclaimed the old pixy thief, 'do you see me today?'

'See you? To be sure I do, as plain as I see the sun in the skies, and I see you are busy into the bargain.'

'Do you so!' cried he. 'Pray with which eye do you see all this?'

'With the right eye to be sure.'

'The ointment! The ointment!' exclaimed the old fellow. 'Take that for meddling with what did not belong to you – you shall see me no more!'

He struck her eye as he spoke, and from that hour till the day of her death she was blind on the right side, dearly paying for having satisfied an idle curiosity in the house of a pixy.

Lame Molly

Two serving damsels declared, as an excuse perhaps for spending more money than they ought upon finery, that the pixies were very kind to them, and would often drop silver for their pleasure into a bucket of fair water which they placed, for the use of those little beings, every night in the chimney corner before they went to bed. Once, however, it was forgotten; and the pixies, finding an empty bucket, whisked upstairs to the maids' bedroom, popped through the keyhole, and began in a very audible tone to complain of the laziness and neglect of the maids.

One of them, who lay awake and heard all this, jogged her fellow-servant and proposed getting up immediately to do what should have been done; but the lazy girl, who did not wish to be disturbed from a comfortable sleep, pettishly declared 'that, for her part, she would not stir out of bed to please all the pixies in Devonshire.' The good-humoured maid, however, got up, filled the bucket, and was rewarded by a handful of silver pennies found in it the next morning. But before that time had arrived, she was very alarmed, as she crept towards the bed, to hear all the elves in high and stern debate, consulting as to what punishment should be inflicted on the lazy lass who would not stir for their pleasure.

Some proposed 'pinches, nips and bobs', others to spoil her new cherry-coloured bonnet and ribbons. One talked of sending her the tooth-ache, another of giving her a red nose; but this last was voted too severe and vindictive a punishment for a pretty young woman. So, tempering mercy with justice, the pixies were kind enough to let her off with a lame leg, which was so to continue only for seven years, when the only cure would be a certain herb growing on Dartmoor, whose long and learned and very difficult name the elfin judge pronounced in a high and audible voice. It was a name of seven syllables, seven being also the number of years decreed for the chastisement.

The good-natured maid, wishing to save her colleague suffering, tried with might and main to bear in mind the name of this potent herb. She said it over and over again, tied a knot in her garter at every syllable (a help to memory then popular) and thought she had the word as sure as her own name. At length she dropped asleep, and did not wake till the morning.

Now, whether her head was like a sieve, that lets out as fast as it takes in, or if trying too hard to remember might cause her to forget, can't be determined; but certain it is, when she opened her eyes, she knew nothing at all about the matter, except that Molly was to go lame on her right leg for seven long years, unless a herb with a strange name could be got to cure her. And lame Molly went, for nearly the whole of that period.

At length (it was about the end of the time) a merry, squint-eyed, queer-looking boy, leapt up one fine summer day, just as she went to pick up a mushroom, and came tumbling head over heels towards her. He insisted on striking her leg with a plant which he held in his hand. From that moment she got well; and lame Molly, as a reward for her patience and suffering, became the best dancer in the whole town at the celebrated activities of May Day on the green.

The enchanted garden

Near a pixy field in this neighbourhood there lived at one time an old woman with a cottage and a very pretty garden, where she cultivated a most beautiful bed of tulips. The pixies, it is traditionally said, so delighted in this spot that they would carry their elfin babies to it, and sing them to rest. Often, at the dead hour of the night, a sweet lullaby was heard, and strains of the most melodious music would float in the air, which seemed to be created by no musicians, other than the beautiful tulips themselves, and while these delicate flowers waved their heads to the evening breeze, it sometimes seemed as if they were marking time to their own singing.

As soon as the elfin babies were lulled asleep by such melodies, the pixies would return to the neighbouring field and there start dancing, making those rings on the green which showed, even to mortal eyes, what sort of gambols had occupied them in the night season.

At the first dawn of light, the watchful pixies once more

sought the tulips and, though still invisible, they could be heard kissing and caressing their babies. The tulips, thus favoured, retained their beauty much longer than any other flowers in the garden; while the pixies breathed over them, they became fragrant as roses; and so delighted at this was the old woman who owned the garden that she never suffered a single tulip to be plucked from its stem.

At length, however, she died, and the heir who succeeded her destroyed the enchanted flowers and converted the spot into a vegetable patch, which so disappointed and offended the pixies that they caused it to wither away; and indeed for many years nothing would grow anywhere in the whole garden. But these sprites, though eager in resenting an injury, were, like most warm spirits, equally capable of returning a benefit; and if they destroyed the product of the good old woman's garden when it had fallen into unworthy hands, they tended the bed of her grave with affectionate care. They were heard in the churchyard lamenting and singing dirges around her tombstone every night before the moon was at the full; for then their high solemnity of dancing, singing and rejoicing took place, to hail the queen of the night when she had completed her silver circle in the skies.

No human hand ever tended the grave of the poor old woman, who had nurtured the tulip bed for the delight of these elfin creatures; but no rank weed was ever seen to grow upon it; the earth was ever green, and the prettiest flowers would spring up without sowing or planting and so they continued to do till it was supposed that the mortal body was reduced to its original dust.

Huccaby

On the left bank of the River Dart, just above Hexworthy Bridge, stands Huccaby Farmhouse, where, several years ago, the presiding genius of the dairy was a buxom lass whose attractions were not unheeded by the youthful swains of the neighbourhood.

But the rivalry for the smiles of the damsel was of a friendly nature, and the passion of her many admirers, though in all probability not deficient in ardour, was not of too deep-rooted a character. They were able to bear up against the disappointment of losing her, for when it at last became known that Tom White, of Post Bridge, was the favoured suitor, the others took a very philosophical view of the matter, and instead of rushing off straightaway to hang themselves from the nearest tree – or, as trees are scarce objects on the moor, taking a fatal plunge in the waters of the Dart – they thought no more about it but quietly left Tom with the field to himself.

Post Bridge is nearly five miles from Huccaby, and as his farm work would not permit him to visit the lady of his love by day, he was forced to content himself with seeing her in the evening, when labour was over. After a hearty evening meal – for Tom did not believe in making love on an empty stomach – he would set out to walk the five miles like a man, and at the end of his meeting with the fair maiden he would trudge back again to his home. A walk of ten miles after a day spent in labour is an undertaking that many men would shrink from; but what is it to a man in love? And the plucky way in which Tom accomplished it, several evenings a week, proved the ardour of his passion. Boldly would he set forth from his home, and his walk over Lakehead Hill and by the rugged rocks of Bellaford Tor was rendered light and easy by the anticipation of the blissful time in store for him, and his journey back was made cheerful by his recollection of it.

One would suppose that a man who could look lightly upon a walk of this kind would be so firm in his determination to win the young lady's hand that nothing would turn him from it. But alas! it was not to be so. One summer night Tom had stayed rather later than usual, and as he strode onward, after mounting the slope behind the house, he saw that the stars were beginning to pale before the coming dawn. He walked rapidly, for he began to think that he would hardly get to bed before the hour when he must rise to go to work, and he was anxious to get home as soon as he could.

Plodding onward, Tom soon reached the slope of Bellaford Tor. As he passed by the walls of the new-takes and approached the tor itself, he fancied he heard sounds of merry voices in the distance. Once or twice he paused to listen, but the sounds were so faint, and the probability of anyone being about at that early hour in such a spot so slight, that he came to the conclusion he had mistaken the sighing of the wind for voices, and pressed on his way.

And now the rocks of the tor began to rise dimly before him, assuming in that uncertain light strange and fantastic shapes. The ground over which he was passing was strewn with granite blocks, and he had to proceed more cautiously. Arrived at the tor, he was threading his way through the scattered rocks with the intention of passing on one side of it, when suddenly sounds similar to those he had previously heard struck upon his ear, but so plainly that he knew he was labouring under no delusion.

Before he could look around him to discover where the sounds came from, their volume increased tenfold, and it was evident that a very merry party was somewhere close at hand. Now it flashed into his mind that he had approached a pixy gathering, and stepping at that instant round a huge granite boulder, he came upon a strange and bewildering sight.

On a small level piece of velvety turf, entirely surrounded by boulders, a throng of little creatures were assembled, dressed in most fantastic costumes. A great number of them had joined hands, and were dancing merrily in a ring, while many were perched upon the rocks around, and all were laughing and shouting with glee. Poor Tom was frightened beyond measure, and knew not whether it was better to proceed or try to retreat. If he could steal away unobserved he might be able to pass on the opposite side of the tor, and this he decided to do. But no sooner had he made up his mind than the little folks spotted him, and, instantly forming a ring round him, danced more furiously than ever.

As they whirled around, Tom was forced to turn round with them, although they danced so rapidly that he was utterly unable to keep up with their frantic movements. Each one, too, was joining in the elfin chorus as loud as his little lungs would enable him, and although they danced and sung with all their might they never seemed to tire. In vain Tom called upon them to stop – his cries only causing the pixies to laugh the merrier – while they seemed to have no intention whatever of stopping their antics. Tom's head began to swing round; he put out his arms wildly, his legs felt as if they would give way under him; yet he could not avoid spinning round in a mad whirl. He would have given anything to stop, and endeavoured in vain to throw himself on the grass; the mad gallop still continued, and poor Tom was compelled to take his part in it.

In the height of the din, the sun began to rise above the ridge of Hameldon, and at the first sight of it the noise suddenly ceased, the little folk instantly vanished among the crevices of the rocks, and Tom found himself lying alone on the moor.

Plucking up his courage, he made his way towards home as fast as he was able, devoutly hoping he might reach it without encountering any more pixies. This he fortunately did, and got to rest without delay.

But alas! the pixies had done more harm than merely worrying a poor mortal; they were the means of the buxom damsel of Huccaby losing her lover. Poor Tom was so frightened at his night's adventure that he made a vow, that he would never go courting any more – and he kept it. It is probable there were people, who were ready to doubt if Tom White ever saw the pixies at all, and were prepared to assign as a reason for his belief that he did so, the probability that he had consumed something a little stronger than water, before leaving his lady-love, and this would account for the spirits getting into his head.

Be that as it may, Tom stoutly declared it was all as he said, and resolutely stuck to his determination of avoiding the fascinations of the fair sex in future.

The pixy at the Ockerry

One evening a woman who dwelt on the moor was pursuing her homeward way, and as darkness began to gather round her she found herself nearing the bridge which spans the Blackabrook at the Ockerry, between Princetown and Two Bridges. When she was within about fifty yards of it, a small figure suddenly ran bounding into the road, and ran leaping and gambolling in front of her towards the stream. She was very much startled at first, and paused, scarcely knowing whether it was better to continue on her way or turn back. She had almost resolved on turning back, thinking it very probable that unless she avoided the frisky little fellow she would be pixy-led, when the recollection that her family were awaiting her arrival made her decide to proceed.

To prevent any such misfortune as being drawn aside from her path by the pixy, she turned her pockets inside out, and also reversed the shawl she was wearing, and plucking up her courage walked boldly on. The pixy had now reached the bridge, and remained jumping from side to side and performing a variety of antics upon it, as if to prevent her crossing, but the dame's courage did not fail her. Having made up her mind not to be deterred, she stepped fearlessly towards the spot where the pixy was, who continued his grotesque movements, leaping about with the greatest agility. As the stout-hearted woman gained the bridge, the little fellow hopped towards her. Suddenly stooping down, she seized the pixy in her hand, popped him into the basket she was carrying, and secured the cover, resolving that instead of running any risk of being pixy-led she would turn the tables and lead the pixy.

The basket was a large one, but the captive being, as she afterwards said, fully eighteen inches in height, there was not much room in it for him to display his agility, so he was forced to lie still. But though still, he was not silent, for immediately the cover of the basket was fastened upon him, he began talking in a very rapid manner, but in so strong a jargon that the good dame was unable to comprehend a word. She however, with her basket on her arm, continued her way, determined not to allow the pixy to frighten her with his gibberish. After a time the little fellow's voice ceased, and his captor imagined he might possibly be tired of talking, or had grown sulky, or perhaps had fallen asleep. She felt curious to know what he was doing, and determined upon taking a peep at her prize. Cautiously raising the cover of the basket about an inch or so, she looked in, when, strange to relate, she found it to be perfectly empty. How the pixy had effected his escape was a mystery, and she could only conjecture that it possessed the power of changing its shape and had contrived to squeeze itself out through the wickerwork.

Though unable long to retain her prize in her possession, the good dame was always able to boast that she had had the courage to capture a pixy.

Jimmy Townsend's sister

In a cottage on the moor lived Jimmy Townsend, a merry fellow, who was always ready for a drink or two with anyone he knew, if he met them at a sheep-shearing feast, or at market in Tavistock; and he was never tired of telling them long stories of his various adventures.

Though Jimmy was not particularly fond of work, he was perfectly unaware of that fact himself. It was not unusual to hear him boast of an evening that he had again 'cheated a 'oss of a day's work.' He was always welcome wherever he went, and the party was sure to be the merriest where he was present. He never allowed anything to trouble him, and was fond of assuring his friends that he 'ded'n want for nothin'' – in fact, he said he was happy as a king, 'although he did live with a pisgie.'

Jimmy Townsend had a sister named Grace – at least everybody spoke of her as his sister, but Jimmy knew better – who lived with him and kept his house tidy; and though Jimmy treated her very familiarly, as though she had been his sister, yet he always insisted that she was 'not a Christian at all, but nothin' but a pisgie.'

Jimmy was many years older than Grace, and said he remembered well when his sister was born, and 'a sweet little thing her was. But,' said Jimmy, 'her wasn'a twelve month old avor her was stole away, an' a pisgie put in her cradle in her place. I knaw 'tis so,' he stated, 'vor her grawed up sich a cross-tempered little thing as you ever zeed, an' whoever's got anything at all to do wi'her will sure to come to some harm.'

Nothing could shake Jimmy's belief. Every little mishap in the household was attributed by him to the 'pisgie', and while he tolerated the presence of Grace, and even felt glad to have her to look after his home, he never regarded her in any other light than as one of the elfin race. 'I never cross her,' he would say, 'vor I knaw I should be wuss off. I let her do as her minds to, and doan't meddle wi' nothin' in the ouze.'

But pixy or not, one thing was certain – the charms of Grace were potent enough to gain the admiration of one Sam Campin, who, disdainful of the warnings offered by Jimmy, boldly pleaded his suit, declaring in his own way that Grace was his idea of perfection, and if she was a pixy, 'it dedn't make no odds!' So it was at last settled that Sam should marry Grace, and one bright morning he tripped off with her to the church, and the parson having performed his office, they returned man and wife.

Jimmy Townsend vowed that it would not be long ere the bridegroom discovered that his life was not likely to wear the rosy hue he had fondly anticipated, for, he said, 'he's got a pisgie for his wive, and I knaw et!' At first, however, things went on pretty well, and Sam Campin had nothing to complain of, and many there were who jeered at Jimmy, calling him a false prophet. But he was not to be shaken in his belief that matters would not turn out well for Sam. 'Wait a bit, wait a bit, an' you'll zee,' he said.

Two or three months passed, and Sam Campin's cow fell sick and died. Not long afterwards, a litter of pigs were found dead one morning and a flock of geese had mysteriously disappeared. 'Dedn' I tell 'ee so?' asked Jimmy of those who had been asking him when Sam's problems were going to start. 'Her's a pigsie an' her's sure to bring harm to whoever's got anything to do wi' her. Bless your saul! I had to keep from meddlin' when I was with her or I should have been in a purty mess o't avor now. But when a man's got her for a wive, how can he help o'comin' to a squabblin' sometimes?'

Things continued to grow worse, and after a time poor Sam Campin had been forced to sell all his worldly possessions, and poverty was staring him in the face. Looking around for some work he could do, he at length decided to become a chimney sweep. It was a job which would not require a great deal of practice in order to be proficient in. The people in the few farm-houses around were not likely to become customers, certainly, for they kept their chimneys free from soot by drawing a bunch of furze up and down them occasionally – which was a quite adequate method and had the great merit of being free. But in the villages on the borders of the moor – Widecombe church-town, Holne, and such like – where there were a few houses of the better class, Sam considered there would be work enough to keep one sweep employed, and so he set manfully about preparing himself for his new vocation.

Jimmy Townsend said nothing – merely shaking his head when the subject was mentioned in his presence, as if to imply that he had no faith in the undertaking.

And now the day arrived on which our sweep was to undertake his first chimney. Armed with his brushes, he made for the house where his services were required, and, on arriving, at once set to work. Those were not the days of brushes with a handle jointed like a fishing rod and capable of reaching through any chimney, no matter what its height, and a great deal of work had to be done by the operator climbing up into the chimney and sweeping down the soot with a brush whose handle was only a few feet long. This needed to be done on the occasion we speak of, and Sam prepared to climb.

It was with some fear that he looked up the black and uninviting cavity, but, shaking this feeling off, up he climbed. Down came the soot as Sam vigorously wielded his brush, and all seemed to be going on well. Suddenly his movements ceased. They called up to him from below. There was no answer. They called again and a faint groan was the response. When they got a light and peered up, it was found that poor Sam had stuck fast in the chimney!

'I toold 'ee so! I toold 'ee so!' exclaimed Jimmy Townsend, when Sam's uncomfortable position was made known to him. 'I knawed how et would be. No good'll ever come to anybody who's got ort to do wi' the pisgies!'

And so it proved, for though rescued from the chimney, Sam was never afterwards able to undertake anything whatever without meeting with some mishap.

The ungrateful farmer

A small farmer once lived on the moor, who was so very poor that he had as much as he could do to keep himself and his family from starving. He cultivated a few fields which had been reclaimed from the waste but the crops were seldom of much value.

One day, on approaching his barn, he heard sounds of laughter and merriment proceeding from within. Going cautiously to the door, he put his ear to the crevice and heard what seemed to be a company of little people busily engaged in threshing corn.

After having listened for some time, he stepped quietly away and remained at work at the other end of the yard until he judged the pixies – for such he knew the little labourers to be – had finished their task. Then, proceeding to the barn once more, he was mightily pleased at discovering what the merry little troop of workers had accomplished for him. They had threshed a goodly quantity of his corn, and having relieved him of the trouble of doing it himself, had given him time for the rest of his work, and by nightfall he found there was as much done as would have taken him nearly two days to perform by himself.

This put him in good humour, and he decided not to go to the barn on the next morning, but to let the pixies have it all their own way. He carried out this resolution, and it wasn't until late afternoon that he approached the barn. On entering it he was met by the same pleasing sight as on the preceding morning. Curiosity now took possession of his mind, and he began to think he should like to see the little people at work. He knew it would be necessary to exercise caution, so he decided on going very early to the barn on the following morning, and waiting in hiding for the arrival of the pixies. This he did, and after a time was delighted at seeing the troop of little people run merrily into the barn, some of them carrying flails (or 'dreshels' as they are called in Devonshire) on their shoulders. Soon all was bustle and noise. The strokes of the flails resounded on the floor, and peals of laughter rang through the old barn, as the active little goblins bent to their task.

The farmer looked on with amazement from his station behind the straw, eagerly gazing at the astonishing scene before him. On a sudden, one of the pixies – a sharp, pert-looking fellow – dropped his flail and cried out in a shrill voice, 'I twit, you twit.' The others looked up, and threw down their flails too. Now the farmer, although he had not been discovered, imagined he had been, and remembering that once the pixies learn they are overlooked they never return to the spot again, was filled with vexation, and as the pert little fellow on the floor once more raised his tiny voice and called out, 'I twit, you twit,' he rushed forth in a temper exclaiming, 'I'll twit 'ee!' upon which the pixies immediately vanished, and never came near his barn any more.

There is an alternative ending to this tale, in which the farmer leaves well alone, instructs his labourers to do likewise, and rapidly makes his fortune.

Rewarding a pixy

On going one morning to his barn to thresh some corn, a moor farmer found that it would not be necessary for him to perform that task, for a sufficient quantity was already threshed and placed in the centre of the floor in readiness for removal. The good man gazed around him in perplexity, utterly unable to comprehend the meaning of what he beheld. The straw was made neatly up into bundles, and stacked on one side; the floor all around the heap of corn had been swept clean, and everything was looking in a perfectly tidy condition.

Not being able to imagine who had done him this piece of service, he hurried across the yard to his house to acquaint his wife with what he had seen, and find out whether she knew anything about it. His wife, on hearing what he had to say, unhesitatingly gave it as her opinion that it was the work of the pixies, in which the farmer, seeing no other probable explanation, acquiesced. He felt mightily obliged to the little folks, as their labour had made it unecessary for him to thresh any corn that day.

The next morning, needing more corn, he headed for his barn with his flail across his shoulder, meaning to work on the threshing floor until dinner time. On opening the door, what was his surprise to find that he had again been helped in his labours, and that on this day, as on the preceding one, there would be no need for him to use his flail. There stood a large heap of corn ready for him to take away, and as he looked at it he was filled with surprise and pleasure, and also with feelings of thankfulness to the kind little pixies who had again lightened his labours so considerably. He hastened once more to the house and told his wife that the same thing had happened again, on hearing which she was as pleased as himself, and as thankful to the pixies.

The good farmer kept thinking about it all that day, and at last decided that he would keep a watch in the barn, and discover in what manner the little people performed their self-imposed task, for he never doubted that it was to the labours of the pixies that he was indebted for what was done.

Accordingly he sat up late that night, and in the small hours of the morning stole out cautiously, and going to his barn, hid himself in the straw. Here he waited very patiently until daylight began to appear, when he heard a rustling sound in one corner of the barn, and peeping out of his hiding place beheld on the floor a single lone figure, who at once started with great rapidity spreading the corn ready for threshing. The tiny sprite then took up the flail which he had brought with him and used it with such lusty good will that very quickly a quantity of corn was threshed. This he swept up into a heap in the centre of the floor, and rapidly making the straw into bundles, placed them against the wall of the barn and disappeared. The astonished farmer hastened from his place of concealment and rushed to his house to inform his better half that he had seen the pixy at work, and the honest couple talked of nothing else during the whole time they sat over their breakfast.

And now the farmer and his wife considered how to reward the pixy for his kindness. The good man had noticed that the pixy wore very dilapidated clothes – in fact they could scarcely be called clothes at all, for the worn-out garments were hanging about him in tatters – so they decided that an appropriate gift to the little fellow would be a new suit. The good lady took out some pieces of material in the most gaudy colours she could find, and a selection was made from them. So busily did she ply her needle that by the time supper was set upon the board she had made the complete suit, and brought them to her good man to hear what he would say about them. He approved very much, praised her skill, and feeling glad he would now be able to provide his little thresher with decent raiment, fell to supper.

After his wife had retired to bed, the farmer sat himself down by the hearth until it was time to go to the barn. Knowing that the pixy would not be likely to appear till dawn, he waited until he judged it to be about an hour before day-break, when he again quietly made his way there, and concealed himself in the same spot he had before chosen, taking care before doing so to place the little suit of clothes on the floor where he knew the pixy would be sure to see them.

Daylight at length began to appear, and at the first faint sight of it the little sprite was seen to make his way from the corner of the barn. The farmer eagerly watched him, picturing to himself the pleasure the little fellow would show at seeing his labours were appreciated, and anxiously looking forward to seeing him working with his flail, perhaps with even greater zeal. The pixy no sooner stepped across the floor than he saw the attractive garments, and pouncing upon them in an eager manner, cast off his fluttering rags and rapidly dressed himself in the new clothes. Glancing down with a look of pride at his little figure, he exclaimed, 'New toat, new waist-toat, new breeches; you proud, I proud; I shan't work any more!' and, almost before the astonished watcher could comprehend what had occurred, he vanished.

He never appeared again, and the farmer was afterwards

always obliged to thresh his corn himself, but he never ceased to regret that he had been the cause of making a pixy too proud to work.

The pixy riders

Some colts belonging to a farmer on the moor, were running in a large new-take. They were needed, so a boy was despatched to fetch them. When he reached the spot where the animals were, he was astonished to find them galloping madly over the ground, while sitting astride on the neck of each was a diminutive rider, urging them on in their wild career, and shouting uproariously. In vain the boy attempted to stop them. Faster and faster the terrified animals flew over the new-take, while their riders twisted their manes and forced them onward among the boulders of granite in a most reckless manner.

At length the pixies, on gaining a corner of the new-take, suddenly threw themselves off their steeds, which, covered with sweat and foam, gathered closely together gazing fearfully around them. Where the pixies went to the boy could not tell, but the skilful manner in which they managed the animals they bestrode convinced him, as he afterwards said, that 'twudn' the fust time that they piskies had been up to thackey!'

Modilla and Podilla

One winter evening the womenfolk of a lonely farmhouse, on the borders of the moor near Brent, were seated at the large kitchen table, busily preparing some good things for supper, for they were about to celebrate some family festival. A huge joint was slowly turning on the spit before the fire, and a most appetising smell pervaded the apartment. The work was going forward briskly, the women concentrating hard on it, when the door was pushed gently open and a little figure made its appearance.

The occupants of the room remained perfectly silent, watching with great curiosity the actions of the intruding pixy, who was a slim little fellow clad in tight pantaloons and a neat jacket of green. He approached the hearth and looked closely at the joint of meat revolving on the spit, and then, as if satisfied, turned away and stared at the various objects within the chimney corner. At length he stood up before the fire, and plucking a single hair out of his head, let it fall into the blaze. This he repeated a number of times, but in a very slow and deliberate manner, the women looking on, quite at a loss to understand such strange behaviour. It was evident that the pixy was unaware of their presence, and, quite at his ease, he continued his hair pulling before the fire.

In the midst of this a tiny voice was heard, calling from outside in a tone of warning as though danger was near, 'Modilla! Modilla!'

The pixy started and instantly called out, 'Podilla! Podilla!'

'Modilla!' repeated the voice, this time in a very peremptory manner.

'Modilla!' responded the elf by the fire, and instantly darted through the doorway.

The women rose and rushed out after him, but the pixy was nowhere to be seen, though the outer door was securely fastened. His companion outside had by some means become aware of the presence of the people in the kitchen, and had at once called him away from a spot where he was likely to run into danger.

The ploughman's breakfast

One beautiful morning a labourer on one of the Dartmoor farms was engaged in ploughing a field. He had started at break of day, and with his team and wooden plough – still called by its own name of 'sull' or 'soll' on the moor – had completed many furrows as the hour for breakfast drew near. The keen moor air had sharpened his appetite to such an extent that he more than once looked wistfully towards the gate of the field, in order to see whether his little son was making his appearance with his morning meal. but the boy was not as yet to be seen, and our labourer, trying to forget his hunger, determined to wait patiently, continuing to plough steadily on, whistling merrily, and calling cheerfully to his team.

In the middle of the field was a huge granite block, which when the enclosure had been reclaimed from the moor had been left where it stood, its size forbidding any attempts to clear it away. As the ploughman passed near this block on his way across the field, he was startled at hearing voices apparently proceeding from beneath it. He listened, and distinctly heard one, in a louder tone than the rest, exclaim, 'The oven's hot!'

'Bake me a cake then,' instantly called the hungry ploughman, in whose mind the very mention of an oven had conjured up thoughts of good food. 'Bake me a cake then.'

He continued his furrow to the end of the field, when, turning his plough, he set out on his return journey. When he approached the rock, what was his surprise and delight at seeing, placed on its surface, a nice cake, smoking hot. He knew at once that this was the work of the obliging little pixies, who evidently had a resort under the rock, and who had taken pity on his hunger, and provided him with his morning meal. Seizing the dainty morsel, and seating himself upon the stone, the ploughman made it disappear almost as fast as the pixies had provided it, but while satisfying his hunger he didn't forget to feel grateful to the kind little people who, about to enjoy their own breakfast, were not unmindful of the wants of a poor labourer.

Jan Coo

At Dartmeet, the east and west branches of the Dart mingle their water, and the course of the united stream, until it leaves the uplands, is through a deep and narrow valley overhung with rugged tors. An observer from one of the heights crowning the sides of the valley identifies the course of the river, as it rushes along its rocky channel, by the white flashes of foam. The grey granite sides of the tors contrast strikingly with the coppices of oak, and the whole scene is one of great wildness.

On the left bank of the river rises the bold conical pile of Sharp Tor, and on the slope of this hill stands a solitary farmhouse called Rubric [now Rowbrook], overlooking the valley below. At this farm a boy was once employed to tend the cattle – a quite inoffensive lad, who fulfilled his duties to the satisfaction of his master.

One evening in the winter season, when he had been nearly twelve months on the farm, he came hurriedly into the kitchen, exclaiming that he had heard someone calling, and imagined that it must be a person in distress. The farm workers who were gathered around the cheerful peat fire rose quickly, thinking it quite likely that some wayfarer had lost his way in the valley. They quickly reached the spot where the boy said he had heard the voice, and paused to listen. Nothing but the sound of the rushing river below met their ears, and the men declared that the boy must have been mistaken. He, however, stoutly asserted that he was not, and as if to bear him out, a voice was suddenly heard, seemingly at no great distance, calling out, 'Jan Coo! Jan Coo!'

The men shouted in reply, at which the voice ceased. Lights were fetched and they searched around the spot, but no traces of anyone could be seen, so after spending some further time in calling, but without obtaining any response, they re-entered the house, not knowing what to think.

The next night came; the men were gathered around the

hearth as before, when the boy rushed in to say that the voice could again be heard. Up jumped the men, and running to the spot to which they had gone the previous night, listened intently. Out of the stillness of the night came the voice, calling again, 'Jan Coo! Jan Coo!' They looked at one another, but stayed silent, waiting until the voice should be heard once more before replying. And once again upon the night air came the cry 'Jan Coo! Jan Coo!' at which they gave a lusty shout, but waited in vain for any response. All was silent, and after trying again by repeated calls to get an answer from the mysterious visitor, they once more sought the warmth of the chimney corner.

''Tis the pisgies, I'll warn,' said an old man as he settled down on his low seat by the fire. 'I've heard mun say that you can't tell mun, when they be calling, from a Christian.'

'Eess, that's what that is, vor sartin; an' us had better let 'em bide, an' not meddle wi'em,' said another, so they all decided to take no further notice of the strange voice, should it be heard again.

And heard again it was. Not a night passed but, as soon as the men were gathered around the fire after their evening meal, the mysterious voice again rang through the valley – 'Jan Coo! Jan Coo!'

The winter had nearly passed away, and the people at the farm were looking forward to the fast-approaching spring, when the lad, with one of the labourers, was mounting the slope that stretched from the house down to the river. It was dusk and they were returning home to their supper, having finished their work for the day. Suddenly the voice was heard in Langamarsh Pit, on the other side of the river, calling as before, 'Jan Coo! Jan Coo!' The boy instantly shouted in reply, when, instead of the calls ceasing as on the occasions when the men had replied to them, they were heard again, 'Jan Coo! Jan Coo!'

Once more the lad shouted, and again there came the same cry, this time louder than before.

'I'll go and see what 'tis,' exclaimed the boy; and before his companion could attempt to dissuade him from it, he had started to run down the hill towards the river. The many boulders in its rocky bed made crossing places at certain points – when the stream was not swollen with the rains – known to those living in the vicinity, and towards one of these the boy made his way. His companion watched him but a short distance, for in the deepening twilight he was speedily lost to view, but as the man continued his ascent of the hill the voice still came from Langamarsh Pit, 'Jan Coo! Jan Coo!' Again as he approached the farmhouse, he could hear it, and as he neared the door the sounds still rang through the valley, 'Jan Coo! Jan Coo!' Gaining the threshold, he paused before entering, with his hand holding the string which raised the latch, and listened for the voice once more. It had ceased.

He waited but no sound broke the stillness of the evening, and seeking the kitchen he told what had happened to those gathered there, who wondered what the lad would have to tell them when he came back. Hour after hour passed away. The boy did not come. The men went down to the river and called him by name, but they received no reply; they waited expecting him to return, but he didn't appear, and as no news of him was ever obtained, and the mysterious voice ceased its nightly calls, they came to the conclusion that he had been spirited away by pixies.

The Chagford pixies

A gentleman, late at night, was driving across the moor to Chagford when he was startled by the merry tinkle of tiny bells. Lights appeared in the meadows close at hand as of thousands of glow-worms shedding their luminous rays on every leaf, while an innumerable company of the small people danced joyfully to the lively music. Every movement of this assembly of fairies was clearly seen by him.

He reined in his horse and watched their merry antics for a considerable time, sitting motionless to catch the spirit of the merry scene. The grass was crowded with myriads of sprites, some waving garlands of tiny wild flowers, roses and bluebells, others joining in the dance, while not a few had climbed up the slender stalks of tall grasses which scarcely bent beneath their feathery weight. All went merrily till the shrill crow of a cockerel rang out on the night air, when suddenly darkness fell. The gorgeous scene with its fantastically attired crowd vanished from the wayfarer's sight.

The villagers assert that on peaceful nights they often hear the echoes of delightful music and the tripping patter of tiny feet issuing from the meadows and hill sides.

The three little pisgies

There was once a fox, who prowling by night in search of prey, came unexpectedly on a colony of pixies. Each pixy had a separate house. The first he came to was a wooden house.

'Let me in, let me in,' said the fox.

'I won't,' was the pixy's reply, 'and the door is fastened.' So the fox climbed to the top of the house, pushed it down, and made a meal of the unfortunate pixy.

The next house was made of unmortared stones. 'Let me in, let me in,' said the fox.

'I won't,' replied the pixy, 'and the door is fastened.' So the fox climbed to the top of the house, pushed it down, and made a meal of the unfortunate pixy.

The third was an iron house. 'Let me in, let me in,' said the fox.

'I won't,' replied the third pixy, 'and the door is fastened.'

'But I bring good news,' said the fox.

'No, no,' answered the pixy, 'I know what you want. You shall not come in here tonight.' That house the fox tried in vain to destroy. It was too strong for him and he went away in despair. But he returned the next night and exerted all his fox-like qualities in the hope of deceiving the pixy. For some time he tried in vain, until at last he mentioned a tempting field of turnips in the neighbourhood, to which he offered to conduct the pixy – who agreed to meet him the next morning at four o'clock.

But the pixy outwitted the fox, for he found his way to the field and returned laden with turnips long before the fox was out of bed. The fox was greatly vexed, and long unable to devise another scheme, until he thought of a great fair soon to be held a short way off, and proposed to the pixy that they should set off for it together at three in the morning.

The pixy agreed, but the fox was again outwitted, for he was only up in time to meet the pixy returning with his fairings [purchases from the fair] – a clock, a crock and a frying pan.

The pixy, who saw the fox coming, got into the crock and rolled himself down the hill; and the fox, unable to find him, abandoned the scent and went away. The pixy went home, but unfortunately forgot to fasten his door. The fox returned the next morning and, finding the door open, went in – when he caught the pixy in bed, put him in a box, and locked him in. 'Let me out,' said the pixy, 'and I will tell you a wonderful secret.'

The fox was at last persuaded to lift the cover, and the pixy, coming out, threw such a spell upon him that he was compelled to enter the box in his turn – and there at last he died.

This curious story appeared in 1846 in the *Athenaeum* (the Victorian equivalent of the *Times Literary Supplement*), in response to a letter from Ambrose Merton, who suggested that popular traditions were worth recording, and proposed an entirely new word to describe their study – 'folk-lore'. The letter produced an enthusiastic response, and this story was submitted as an example of a tale about pixies then current in the West Country. No mention was made at the time, or in subsequent letters, of its similarity to the nursery story of the three little pigs. I have found no version of the pig story until 1849, three years after this appeared, but that is not to say they do not exist.

'Pixy' was pronounced 'pisgy' or 'pigsy', so confusion with pigs was possible – but which came first, the pigs or the pixies? The version here has lost its punch line, since the clock and the frying pan should have a function in the story, and the 'spell' is an unsatisfactory solution. Pixies are perhaps more likely to live in houses than pigs, and they must certainly use 'turnup' which (meaning swede) is an essential ingredient in Cornish pasties.

The old tales of the pixies have a certain robustness about them, but in the nineteenth century genteel people began to hijack the stories, and make them sentimental. We include the following tale, which has all the appearance of having been invented by a Victorian lady, to show the contrast.

The fairy wedding

Once upon a time the pixy prince was going to wed Princess Halfa, who lived on the topmost bough of an apple tree, out of the reach of a witch, who dwelt amongst the roots and kept watch on her actions. The princess dared not set foot to ground until she was married; and the witch wanted her to marry her son Brandhu, who lived in a cave, and smelted all the tin which the 'nuggies' [knockers] brought him. The nuggies and the pixies did not speak to one another just then, and the Princess Halfa would have nothing to say to Brandhu.

The wicked old witch winked her wicked old eyes and said the wedding should not come off.

Now it should be known that, when a pixy prince married, his bride was bathed in milk and then anointed with the finest cream. The pixies had the cream all ready, and the old witch blew upon it and turned it sour.

Then the pixies prepared the cream a second time, and the old witch turned it sour again.

They prepared it a third time, and she did it again. 'The pixy prince shall never wed the Princess Halfa,' said she. The princess was in the tree waiting, and knew not what to do. So she sighed, and cried, and wrung her hands.

It was early in the spring, about the time of the opening of the apple blossoms. The princess cried louder and louder, until a pink blossom opened and out stepped her pixy prince, carrying in a crystal bowl the clotted cream which had been made by fire, and would not be soured by the witches' breath.

Then the princess anointed herself, and took the pixy's hand, and they jumped to the ground together, and passed the old witch sitting by the roots of the tree, but without power now, for the cream had been made by fire.

The pixies were all friendly with the people, who loved them and took them into their houses, and there never was any rejoicing unless the pixies were there also; and they taught the maidens how to make cream by fire, which they never would have found out of themselves, for before the cream will rise water must cover the bottom of the pan.

Whoever wants clotted cream must use fire and water, and the secret of making it was the gift of the pixies.

Tavistock abbey and the pixies

The old abbots of Tavistock seem to have waged war on the pixies in their neighbourhood. Perhaps they knew them to be representatives of the old religion. But it was not always a one-sided battle.

The abbey produced a noted liqueur, just as other abbeys still do today. This was unusual, in that it was flavoured with heather, and it was a great secret known to only two men at any one time. When one man died, the survivor revealed the secret to a new man. Even the abbots did not know the secret, although they had a plentiful supply, in order to assure themselves that standards were being maintained. Tavistock Abbey thrived mightily, and its abbots were fat and cheerful men.

Abbot John, however, went to war with the pixies. He vowed to drink no more 'heather wine' until he had driven out the pixies from all the parishes and lands under his jurisdiction. The pixies laughed, and took up the challenge. When the abbot was handed a jug of water, they turned it into heather wine. When he passed the distillery, they led him inside and played terrible tricks on him, so that he got into trouble. Even after a great draught of heather wine, taken in all innocence under the impression it was water, when he started to nod in his chair they tickled his nose and his ears, so that he burst out cursing in English and Latin. The monks who heard these outbursts concluded that he had lost his wits, and was possessed by a devil. (We might have mistaken him for an alcoholic).

This continued until one day a pilgrim from the Holy Land came to the abbey. He had learned much in Syria and from the hermits in the desert, and to him the abbot told all.

'It is indeed the evil one, and he must be exorcised,' said the pilgrim promptly.

So there was a High Mass in the chapel, and all the brethren marched around the boundaries of the abbey lands, chanting and sprinkling with holy water, and cursing the pixies with bell, book and candle – and from that day the abbot was troubled no more.

News spread that the pixies had been entirely cleared from the abbey lands. A pixy-cross was set up. Even today, although the abbey is in ruins and all its lands sold, no pixy dares to come near it by day or night. If a man should become pixy-led, the spell is immediately broken once he comes onto the former abbey lands, or into its churchyard.

Tom Kiss-the-Leek

When Tom Bovey was coming back from the fair, he saw a fairy all dressed in green inside a fairy ring. Quick as a flash, he picked her up, but very tenderly, and when he got home he woke up his wife and told her, as well as he could in his excitement, that he had in his pocket the loveliest maiden that ever man clapped eyes on.

Tom's wife said nothing, but watched Tom tie the fairy to the bedpost with his braces, which was an unkind enough way to treat her. Tom fell asleep, and the next morning he saw a great big leek staring him in the face. So he asked his wife what it meant, and she said it was the fairy queen he'd brought home last night, and made such a to-do about.

Then the truth dawned upon him, and he felt ashamed, and took the leek and threw it in the garden. Now, whether Tom was still not quite sober, or whether his tale was true, I cannot say, but the moment that leek touched the fresh earth it turned back into a fairy, and there sprang out of the flowers around it, and from the leaves and everywhere, thousands and thousands of fairies, who encircled their princess and danced off with her, singing, 'We've got her again, we've got her again.'

Tom went back in and told his wife, and they went back and searched the garden but there was no leek and no fairy to be found, only the pig which had got out of its sty, and they drove it back.

When the story was told, their neighbours said the pig had eaten the fairy, and that Tom had kissed the leek.

LIGHT AFTER DARKNESS

LIGHT AFTER DARKNESS

CHIEF RANAMI ABAH

First published in England 1992

Published by LEWIS MASONIC
Ian Allan Regalia Ltd, Coombelands House, Coombelands Lane,
Addlestone, Surrey KT15 1HY, England who are part of the Ian Allan Group of Companies.

British Library Cataloguing in Publication Data

Abah, Ranami
Light After Darkness
I. Title
366
ISBN 0-85318-192-6

Phototypeset and printed by Ian Allan Printing Ltd, Coombelands House,
Addlestone, Weybridge, Surrey KT15 1HY.

CONTENTS

LIST OF PLATES

LIST OF LINE ILLUSTRATIONS

FOREWORD

A comprehensive study of Freemasonry is always to be welcomed. Such works are written and published at regular intervals but in most cases the authors have been initiated under the English Constitution or under one of the many Grand Lodges of the United States of America. So it is particularly pleasing to have a new work which is written by a brother who was initiated in, and is a Past Master of, a lodge under one of the District Grand Lodges of the Grand Lodge of Scotland — in Lodge Faith No 1271 of Nigeria, which is one of the most senior lodges in that most masonically progressive country.

Brother Chief Ranami Abah has obviously spent much time in researching his subject and in writing his conclusions on varying aspects of Freemasonry. These range from symbolism and the masonic landmarks to the Hiramic legend, and he deals with the subject matter of each at length. His views in the chapter on 'Masonry and Religion' should, perhaps, be conveyed to the hierarchy of all religions, and certainly to the Methodist, Baptist, English and Scottish Protestant churches, each of which has expressed anxiety in recent years about their members being freemasons.

This book is commended to members of the Craft of Constitutions throughout the world as it will, without doubt, cause readers to reflect more deeply on many facets of the Craft. Brother Chief Ranami Abah is to be congratulated on the results of his labours.

G. Jerdan
Chairman of the Publications Committee of
the Grand Lodge of Scotland

Plate A: *Bro Chief Ranami Abah, ABIDIFENI III, Hon GDC, PDGDC.*

ABOUT THE AUTHOR

CHIEF RANAMI ABAH, ABADIFENI III

BSc (Est Man), LLB, FRICS, FNIVS, PM Lodge Faith 1271 SC, Hon DGSW, PDGDC, Hon GDC
Substitute District Grand Master Rivers Masonic Zone

Chief Ranami Abah is a man of varied experiences. He is a Chartered Surveyor and Valuer in private practice but with considerable earlier Civil Service Experience at the Senior Level; where he had been Principal Lands Officer for the Federal Government of Nigeria.

He started his working career as a teacher in different categories of schools and colleges helping to mould the character of children and young people.

He started his educational career in Nigeria, attending various schools and colleges and attained his higher education both at the University of Science and Technology Kumasi, Ghana, and the College of Estate Management, University of London, with post graduate working experience both at the London County Council and the Basildon Development Corporation, Basildon, Essex.

He has also been a keen politician who believes in the creation of a confederal democracy as a centre for the unification of all faiths and creeds by the recognition of their differences just as Masonry has done with different religions. He had held the rank of Deputy National Chairman of the ruling party of the Federal Republic of Nigeria.

He is widely travelled and visited practically every part of the world attending masonic meetings whenever he has been able to do so. He has been in Freemasonry for over 20 years, with particular interest in masonic research and charities which he has found to be the most fulfilling of his endeavours.

He has found the desire for the understanding and awareness of the real import and total substance of Freemasonry a living analysis that constitutes a continuous search for all who are freemasons, and this book is dedicated to that analysis and search, and the memory of his late wife, Mrs Alice Elizabeth Clinton Ranami Abah.

1992

PREFACE

Indeed, this book has been written under special conditions of self-exile and solitude, arising from a military coup in Nigeria in 1983, while I was on holiday in Cyprus. I found myself unable to return to Nigeria by virtue of my political position; I was in the circumstances quite fortuitously given a perfect setting in London to reflect on the issues that now constitute *Light After Darkness* in confirmation of our belief that all our actions are guided by His fatherhood, His love, and His will which must at all time give us inner satisfaction.

I am extremely grateful to my mother Lodge, Faith No 1271 SC for giving me birth. I am equally eminently grateful to Bro Chief HM Spiff ADA VII and Bro G. Hartlay-Cowan for proposing and sponsoring me into Freemasonry, and Bro Love D. Jaja for grooming and nurturing me in the ceremonials, rituals, and general understanding of the principles and tenets of Freemasonry.

In the course of compiling this book, I have received assistance and guidance from several distinguished masons and more particularly from Chairman of the Publications Committee of the Grand Lodge of Scotland, and the Grand Secretary. Without wishing to mention the names of all others, I place on record that I am truly appreciative and grateful.

Ranami Abah

INTRODUCTION

'In the bond of Masonry, the heritage of our backgrounds, whether academic, royal, financial, political, cleric, Christian, Hindu, Muslem, professional, technical, scientific, etc is submerged by the common desire for the hidden knowledge of our place and role in creation, and the wonderful manifestations of the Almighty Architect's plan.'

Light After Darkness is the fulfilment of a challenge that has been with me for all the years I have been a mason — the challenge of understanding the real substance of Freemasonry. I am sure I have not found all the answers for no-one can, but if by this modest effort I have managed to stimulate further thoughts on the subject of Freemasonry, then I shall have achieved that fulfilment no matter how small.

Every candidate finds his motivation for becoming a freemason from circumstances peculiar to him and, when eventually he is admitted, he finds the Order useful or disappointing, or even unnecessary, depending on his motivation and the level of his desire for subsequent awareness and enlightenment as mentioned against his expectations for material rewards and benefits. Masons regard themselves as brothers, and accept that 'brotherly love' is one of the three grand principles upon which the Order is founded, the other two being Relief and Truth. As it is a natural tendency for us to expect material benefits flowing out of love from our natural brothers, so it is meet and proper for each mason to expect support and assistance from his Masonic brother as a matter of course. This is in accordance with the five points of fellowship which remind us to succour the weakness and relieve the necessities of our brethren as far as may fairly be done without detriment to ourselves and our connections.

Apart from the qualification that we are only to fulfil this obligation as far as may be done fairly without detriment, we are equally reminded that Freemasonry is *not* a benefit society. It is therefore the ability of each individual mason to maintain a just medium between his expectations of material benefits and his desire for awakening and enlightenment that would determine not only his advancement but also his quality as a mason.

I did not have the privilege of growing up in a masonic family. My family was devoutly Christian, of the Anglican faith. I saw masons in my youth always at a distance, either during funeral ceremonies or on their way to masonic meetings, their insignia being the 'little black box' which I regarded as the repository of the mysteries associated with these men who were invariably over middle-age and dressed in black for the purpose of attending meetings that were held only at night. The totality of all this conjured up in my young mind a strong sensation of curiosity and fear, leading me to regard masons as both mystic and supernatural, even evil. Indeed, I could not completely divorce my mind from these sentiments until several years later, when I was privileged to make one or two friends who were masons. Thus I find it difficult even today to blame those people outside the Order who are deluded about the goings-on in Freemasonry, as what they need is understanding of the Order.

The elements of my motivation were therefore:

(a) curiosity;

(b) A desire for some status symbol which might be both social and mystical; and

(c) a basic interest in all things spiritual and religious.

I found on becoming a mason that my motivation found fulfilment rather in the challenge that the Order presents to every member, for Freemasonry is an institution that presents a challenge in both form and content to its true adherent 'at every turn' from one degree to the next. No human mind that is alive can fail to be awakened by the challenges of the excellence of the lectures at workings, the grandeur of the ceremonials, the perfection and inspirational value of the language of the rituals, the humility of the stewards at banquet, no matter how elevated their social status outside the lodge; the challenge of the ignorance and lack of knowledge of some masons, the challenge of the rectitude of life or even the lack of it in the life of some of its adherents and, above all, the challenge of understanding the real import and total substance of the Craft which is veiled in allegory to make its tenets and principles a living science by the pattern of our lives.

I believe that it is the search for answers to these challenges that leads us to a realisation of the need for that purity and excellence of our life and actions, rather than the hope for reward, that keeps men of such differing backgrounds in one common and indissoluble bond. For, in this bond, the heritage of our backgrounds, whether academic, royal, financial, political, cleric, Christian, Hindu, Muslem, professional, technical, scientific, etc is submerged by our common desire for the hidden knowledge and truth of our place and role in creation, and the wonderful manifestations of the Almighty Architect's plan which Masonry strives to teach. We suddenly gain an inner awareness that sorrow, happiness, solitude, etc are all simply emotions that arise from acts and situations in fulfilment of the grand design of the will of the Creator, which must at all times give us inner satisfaction. The circumstances that led to my writing *Light After Darkness* bear an incontrovertible testimony to my belief and convictions.

It is the analysis of the search for the real import and total substance of Freemasonry which is anchored in the unity of God, the futurity of life and the brotherhood of man, and expressed masonically as faith, hope and charity, that constitutes the central theme of this book. An understanding and awareness of this central theme further leads us to an acceptance of the fact that all our actions are guided by His fatherhood, His Love and His will which again are symbolically expressed in Masonry by the VSL, the Square and the Compasses. This guidance eventually leads us to an understanding of our real purpose and place in life by seeking answers to the questions, 'What am I, whence came I and whither go I?'.

I have therefore endeavoured to look at the symbols, ornaments, allegories, ceremonies, etc as necessary components of our relationship with the general theme. I have also tried to examine any interconnecting links between Masonry and the ancient mysteries and cultures, and whether these are also traceable to this common theme. I have also examined the real substance of Freemasonry, religion, Christianity and the church in relation to this general theme.

I am conscious that thoughts on a subject such as this can only be based on inner awareness, and I am prepared to accept my faults. This work aims at setting no standards for the postulates contained in it, but offers ideas from a personal conviction, thus creating a nucleus for idealisation of certain aspects of the philosophy of our Order. Even if my thoughts and ideas may be controversial or, in certain respects, open to question, I shall have succeeded in my attempt if these ideas have generated further thoughts on the main substance of Freemasonry, in the search for Universal truth and the unity of God.

1

THE BEAUTIES OF TRUE GODLINESS

Embedded with the 'CENTRE' is the divine knowledge that leads to the realisation of our relationship with the Deity, and the discovery and joyful utilisation of this knowledge constitute the BEAUTIES OF TRUE GODLINESS.

FROM TIME IMMEMORIAL and through all ages and lands there has existed a fundamental belief that an inner or Divine degree of knowledge may be acquired or revealed to human beings under certain conditions. This knowledge is invariable related to the nature and destiny of the soul of man and its relationship to a Deity. This is the fundamental principle from which all religions spring; but Masonry, not being a religion, concerns itself with the nature of the belief and not its form.

The secrets of the inner being of man and the divine knowledge that leads to the discovery of our relationship with the 'DEITY' are embedded in the 'CENTRE' or the core of our soul which is the spirit. The discovery and joyful utilisation of this knowledge constitute 'THE BEAUTIES OF TRUE GODLINESS'.

Masonry strives to teach the attainment of this knowledge and the application of its principles and tenets in our daily lives. It is recognised however that these inner values being of a spiritual nature are incommunicable. They transcend communication by word of mouth, but are capable of manifestation through our way of life and therefore can be felt and assimilated through the right light radiations, but in the main can only be attained through personal endeavour.

The Great Mysteries

All the great mysteries of the ancients, including the great uncodified African mysteries and cultures, some of which were regarded as pagan — *Osokolo, Angulama, Nom Awo, Fenibeso, Okedu,* etc have been in search of the same doctrine of Divine truth as the 'Hidden Wisdom'. The ancient mystery orders adopted certain methods of teaching and protecting this wisdom. Indeed, the practice of some of these mysteries and cultures has arisen from a high level of inspiration and conscious development and awareness of our attachment, even to the plane of animistic substantiality which creates the opening up and reception of our spirit guides, which is a stage in our evolution to the understanding of the unity of God through the radiation of His will.

Many mystery orders have flourished in their time and gone into oblivion. Masonry, which now follows in the footsteps of the mystery orders, can only survive if it clings to the more sustaining elements contained therein in its search for eternal truth, wisdom and perfection. In our inadvertent lack of care, the desire for masonic knowledge may be damaged seriously by the lack of masonic instruction and inadequate facilities. The Craft could therefore run the risk of gravitating towards hollow rituals, rites and symbols that will not sufficiently attract and retain enlightened minds. It is becoming clearer day by day that declining emphasis on the expatiation of the mysteries of the Craft constitutes a serious deficiency in our system. To keep it alive and maintain the beauties, we must recognise the nature of the Craft and strive to maintain a just balance between its outward visible part, the intermediate intellectual part, and the inner spiritual part, for the 'science' or 'royal art' known as the Craft contains more than the inculcation of the practice of every moral and social virtue.

The Masonic Content of the Beauties

The secrets of our inner being are said to be embedded in the Centre and Craft Masonry gives positive indications of the need to unravel these secrets in all the degrees practised.

In the first degree, the invocation of the blessing of TGAOTU is particularly exemplary: 'Endow him with the competence of Thy Divine Wisdom, that assisted by the secrets of our masonic art, he may be better enabled to display the beauties of true godliness'. No one need doubt that attainment of the beauties of true godliness lies with spiritual development. The candidate is here further described as being in a state of darkness, worthily recommended and approved in open lodge and humbly soliciting to be admitted into the mysteries and privileges of ancient Freemasonry. In addition, he has to be a free man and of mature age. He also has to believe in a Supreme Ruler of the

Plate B: *Bro Sir James W. McKay, Right Worshipful Past Grand Master Mason.*

universe. The mysteries and privileges that demand these stringent prerequisites for participation could not just be charity, benevolence, relief and truth, etc which can be fully practised and experienced outside the Craft. There must be something more, surely. It is that something more which Masonry is dedicated to inculcate in those who profess the Craft, and it is the discovery and practice of that something which constitute the 'BEAUTIES OF THE TRUE GODLINESS'.

The rough ashlar stage of masonic conception concerns itself with the rituals and ceremonials, the symbols and allegories, and the pleasures of the festive board. But that is not Masonry in the concept considered here.

In the second degree the admonition in the SE charge is particularly exemplary. 'You will now be permitted to extend your researches into the more hidden mysteries of the Craft.' This confirms the 2° as the beginning of the inward development of the mason, symbolized also by the point of the compasses over the square on the VSL, and the lowering of the flap on the rectangular portion of the apron in certain constitutions. It also confirms the fact that the Craft, being an inner awakening, is a matter of individual inner understanding. No man can teach it.

In the third degree, the master's quest at the opening is particularly exemplary: 'Whence came you?', 'Whither are you directing your course?' and 'What inducement have you . . .?' to seek for that which was lost, *ie* the genuine secrets of a MM. These can only refer to the beauties of true godliness, the inner meaning of life. 'Where do you hope to find them?' With the centre, 6 the spirit. When Masonry is understood in this way as a system of moral philosophy expressed in ceremonial drama, then practised in that way, we leave behind us the rough ashlar concept and stage. It is then recognised to be a system that attempts to provide the answers to the three great questions posed by all religions and ancient mystery orders:

WHAT AM I? WHENCE CAME I? WITHER GO I?

the last two of which are amply asked by the RWM at the opening of the lodge in the 3°.

From the foregoing have grown a series of other concepts that indicate the beauties of true godliness. Masons assert that they are directing their course to the west to seek for that which was lost. It is also known that physically the west is the area where the rays of the sun, in its daily course, are at their lowest, and the light pressure from that point least intense. Philosophically, there is a similarity between this and the theory of creation of man. That the spirit germ in its weakness, though conscious, must manifest in an area where the light pressure from above allows its development for upward ascent from whence it came.

The square movement of a Mason from west to east is a further symbolic illustration of the path of man's spiritual growth in creation. It is recognised that the 'mystic science' or 'royal art' known as the Craft deals with the secrets and mysteries of our being. It is this art or craft that deserves protection against profanation and not the general order of the Craft. To maintain the beauties, therefore, it is restricted to minds that are prepared for its reception, *ie* the reception of the universal truth.

In our daily lives the beauties of true godliness cannot be said to be complete until we are able to practise the basic social and moral virtues of brotherly love, relief and truth as these are the cardinal principles that make up the brotherhood of man in conformity with the pure doctrine of love.

Even though relief to the poor and distressed is acknowledged to be a cardinal principle of the Craft, it is sometimes not realised that distress can be spiritual, physical and financial. Masonry as practised today does not minister sufficiently to the distressed in spirit, which is the central core of the institution. Social benevolence seemingly is given too much emphasis today to the detriment of the desired spiritual nurture.

Masonry is sometimes aptly described as the philosophy of the spiritual life of man. This is the truth beneath the definition, 'a peculiar system of morality veiled in allegory and illustrated by symbols'. It is the recognition of man as a human being in ceremonial drama and illustrated by symbols. It is not only a recognition of man, but a recognition of man as *a human being*. It is only the spirit that makes man a human being, for without it he would be one other animal. It is therefore little wonder that man became a human being only after he had received the breath of God as recorded in the VSL, the breath of God being his spirit.

In similar manner, 'The Sacred Symbol' in Masonry alludes to the Divine Spirit in us — the Spirit which after purification is revealed through contemplation and enlightenment, that vital and immortal principle whose rising in the human breast brings peace and consolation to the faithful and obedient among men.

As a further illustration of the common core of wisdom and knowledge that permeates all things masonic, we find that *Hiram* in Hebrew means *Guru*, teacher of 'supreme knowledge', divine light and wisdom, and the liberty that comes with it. But this knowledge is only for the perfected man.

Because the path towards the attainment and maintenance of the beauties of true godliness is so intricate and not even dependent on education or intellectualism, but rather on individual endeavour, we find that primitive man, no matter how childish or intellectually undeveloped he had been, had a higher perception than is experienced today. Modern man has ceased to be childlike through the development of the intellect and has become spiritually indolent.

Masonry believes that life begins with the acceptance of the spirit in an undeveloped form and that once a child is born his spiritual progress must be based on the principles enunciated by the Craft, depending on his personal endeavour in order that the philosophical significance of the rituals in the 3° may be fulfilled, namely

(a) the immortality of life after physical death and

(b) death unto sin and self and a new birth unto righteousness — which is spiritual re-awakening.

2

SYMBOLISM OF THE SQUARE

By due application and contemplation we are enabled to lift the veil of symbolism and realise that the various implements of our profession are emblematical of our conduct in life and are intended to implant in our memory and behaviour wise, and serious truths, if we so desire.

MASONRY IS DESCRIBED as a peculiar system of morality veiled in allegory and illustrated by symbols. This is particularly appropriate for the Craft in its speculative form. It is a science in which every character, figure and emblem depicted in a lodge has a moral tendency and serves to inculcate the practice of every moral and social virtue and ennoble the lives of all those who truly profess it.

To be initiated into this system of morality, which is so veiled and illustrated, the candidate is described as being in a state of darkness, humbly soliciting to be admitted into the mysteries and privileges of ancient Freemasonry.

Generally, to the initiated in all religions or mystery orders there can be no secrets. The Craft being the science of understanding the role of man in creation, we must be spiritually initiated so that the mysteries may unfold before our eyes. The first stop would therefore appear to be a joyous striving towards an understanding of the various imports of the symbols of the science, for how can one profess to understand the science without knowledge of its symbols and emblems?

Such is the peculiar nature of Masonry, and such is the challenge it throws, particularly in the 2°, when candidates are admonished 'You are now at liberty to extend your researches into the more hidden mysteries of the Craft'. This is a challenge which should motivate any true mason who believes the Craft to be the progressive science it is. Indeed, it is one of the challenges that have motivated me to put some of my thoughts on paper, no matter how ordinary they may sound.

I believe that the light a mason receives in the 1° together with the assistance of the square prepares his mind for the reception of truth and wisdom as indeed it should to every true mason.

As we look around us in a normal lodge room, otherwise known as the temple, how many of us are able to recognise the symbols that are physcially present in the temple by way of furniture, jewels and ornaments? Even among those who can recognise them by virtue of long experience and association, how many of them in fact understand the mystic import behind the symbols? In other words, how many are able and willing to lift the veil of symbolism and realise that the various implements of our profession are emblematic of our conduct in life and are intended to implant in our memory and behaviour wise, and serious truths? Can we really describe ourselves as masons before attaining that stage which we must reach by application and contemplation.

What is a Square?

Generally from the point of view of description as an instrument, there is no divergence between the operatives and the speculatives, for the square which is morally applied by the speculatives is derived from the practice of the operatives. Indeed, some generality is discoverable between the teachings of the old operatives and the speculative application of the square as a working tool of the modern Craft as will be observed from the following quotation, *I will strive to live with love and care upon the level by the square.* This was an inscription of an old brass square dated 1517 discovered in 1830 at the rebuilding site of Baal Bridge in Limerick, Ireland by the architect.

Masonically, a square is described as an angle of 90° or the fourth part of a circle. There are other general descriptions which do not basically depart from this. It is also described as being made up of two arms enclosing a right angle where the arms meet, and may be used to measure squareness, to try and adjust rectangular corners of buildings, and assist in bringing rude matter into due form or alignment. To a large extent this is a description that applies to the square of the operative stone mason, which is intended as a test of regularity. It is also described as an instrument used by the craftsman in proving both his materials and the regularity of the structure during construction as he is concerned with practical building in proper manner.

The square is also described as an instrument which is intended purely to test the accuracy of the sides of a stone and to see that its edges subtend the same angle of 90°, *ie* to bring rude matter into due form. When the arms, whether equal or not, are graduated, it becomes

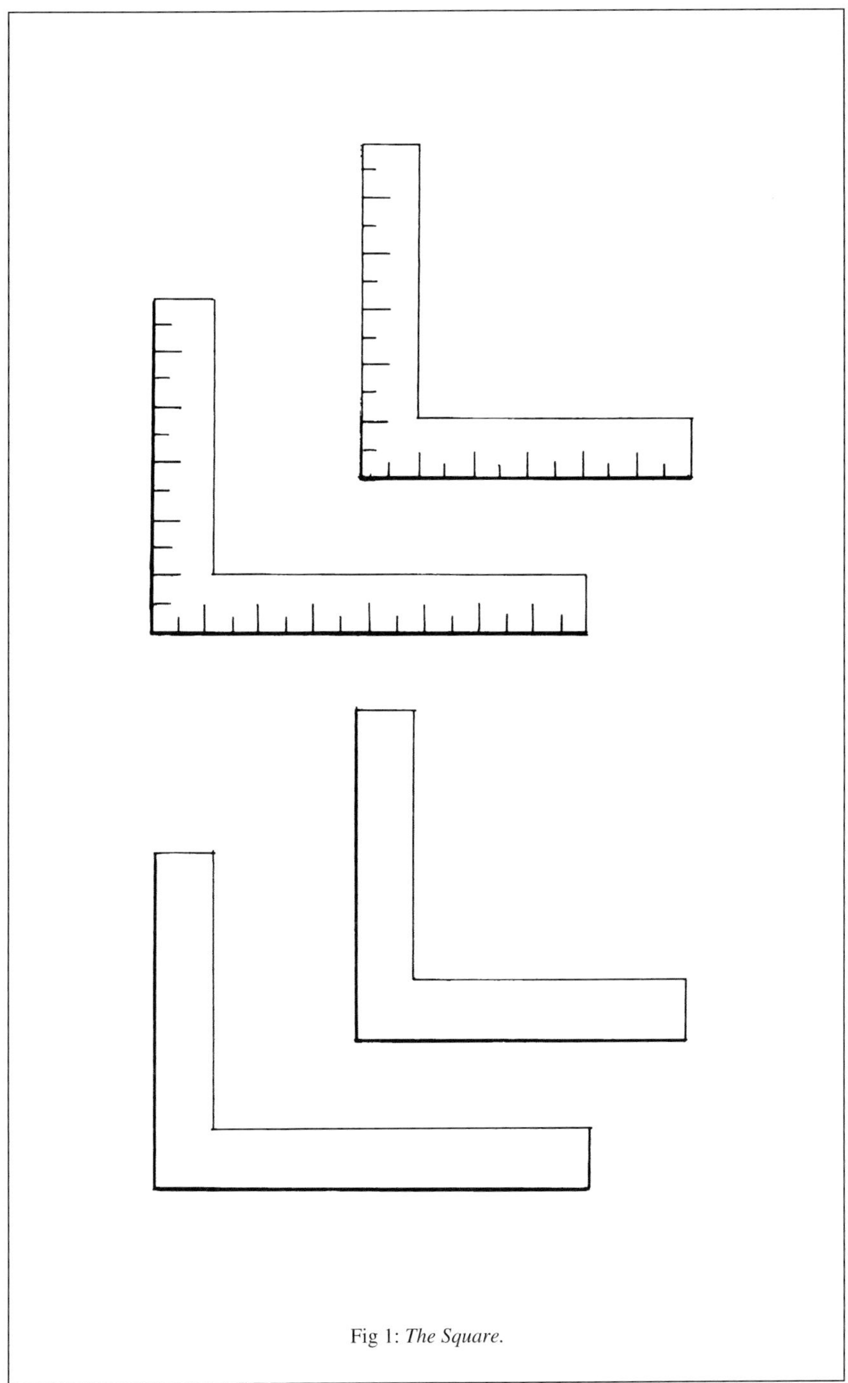

Fig 1: *The Square.*

an instrument for measurement, and when in this state one arm is longer than the other, then it becomes the carpenter's square.

The Square and its From

The history of both the operative and speculative masons shows the adoption of two basic forms of the square, namely the square with equal arms and the square with unequal arms. In speculative Masonry however, the more or less universal adoption of the square with equal arms seems to have come in the 1820s shortly after the union of the English Grand Lodges. The difference in form has not been of any particular significance as the import has always been the same and any significance outside this is merely historical.

French masons, especially under the Grand Orient, have almost universally maintained the phenomenon of the carpenter's square by having one arm longer than the other, a view accepted by the Revd J. L. Lawrence in the *Perfect Ashlar.*

It is also interesting to note that the type of square first used up to the 1830s was the gallows type as portrayed by Klein and Meeson in their expositions. In medieval lodges, the letter 'G' was said to be depicted by a square of the gallows type with unequal arms and similar in shape to the *gamma* or G of the Greek alphabet. This symbol also stood for justice, one of the great characteristics of God as expressed in His will. In expressing these views the Revd J. S. M. Ward believes that it is this symbol that should be placed in the centre of the lodge combining the square itself and the representation of geometry.

American masons on the other hand, following the incorrect delineations of Jeremy L. Cross, have in addition to preserving the equality of the length of the arms, graduated it in inches which makes it an instrument for measurement, which it is not, although modern squares seem to be calibrated as instruments of measurement for use at school or at the engineering shop.

Be that is it may, masons attach significance mainly to the import and application of the square and not its form, for even the term square is something of a misnomer as the symbol in question is but the two adjacent sides of the figure square.

Masonic Application

The square in speculative masonry is generally a symbol of masonry applied in several ways. To the neophyte, it presents itself as one of the three great though emblematical lights in Freemasonry. 'Having been restored to the blessing of material light, let me direct your attention to what we consider the three great, though emblematical lights in Freemasonry (1°ob). The square is then here described as being responsible for the regulation of our actions.

To the FC it is an established fact in all masonic ceremonial practice that the square, the second of the great emblematical lights in Freemasonry, is the special symbol of the 2°, for the whole of the degree is based on the use of the square. It is first, the emblem of his admission into that degree, charging him to act upon the square with all mankind and more particularly with a brother freemason. Then it is next presented to him as a mark of his progress in Freemasonry for, the changed relationship between the square and compasses on the VSL marks the beginning of the candidate's understanding of the hidden mysteries and his spiritual re-awakening or consciousness.

It is next presented to him as one of his working tools, reminding him of both its operative and speculative applications, namely 'To adjust all rectangular corners and to assist in bringing rude matter into due form, to regulate his actions by the masonic rule and line, and to harmonise his conduct with the principles of morality and virtue'.

It is very significant that in this degree the JW at the opening of the lodge asserts to the RWM that he should be proved by the square, and this is followed by a request for the brethren to prove themselves accordingly, which makes the square a symbol of worthiness as a Fellow Craft.

Indeed, the three-fold sign of this degree is even considered by masonic writers as a combination of many squares, and it is even possible to conceive that this sign is an attempt to form the letter G, standing for geometry, the special study of this degree, in which the square is of paramount importance. The letter G being symbolic at the centre of the lodge shows that the FC is at the mid-point of his spiritual progress (C. F. W. Dyer). The old lectures tell us that although the sacred volume is derived from God to man in general, the square belongs to the whole Craft. As the VSL is essentially the Great Light with reference and relevance to the initiate, so is the square to the Fellow Craft.

To the Master Masons and to the Craft in general, the square is the official emblem of the Master of the Lodge, and at the same time it is one of the movable jewels of the lodge, inculcating the useful lessons of morality, truthfulness and honesty. Indeed, so universal is the acceptance of this concept of morality, truthfulness and honesty in relation to the square, that it has fund its way into colloquial language as one of the masonic influences on the world outside.

To the Craft, also generally in Craft ceremonials, all secrets of all the Craft degrees are communicated while the candidate symbolically assumes the posture of the square with his feet, which in the 1° is clearly indicated as being emblematical of the rectitude of his actions. Having considered the application of the square in the different stages of the Craft, it will be necessary to consider the moral import of the square as a masonic symbol.

The Symbolic Import of the Square

The main symbolic import of the square is contained in its masonic description as being responsible for the regulation of our actions, to adjust all rectangular corners and to assist in bringing rude matter into due form, to regulate our actions by the masonic rule and line and to harmonize our conduct with the principles of morality and virtue.

The square therefore represents the lower nature of man which has to be polished and adorned by the principles of morality, truthfulness, honesty and virtue for its upward ascent. The rude matter is emblematically the character and actions of each individual mason, and the building which should be truly square is the structure of his life illuminated in the 1° for the reception of truth and wisdom, under the guidance of the principles of the square in the progressive passage from the 2° to the 3°.

It is masonically emblematic of the rectitude of our actions in our daily lives and for that reason the secrets of each degree in Craft Masonry are imparted while the candidate symbolically assumes the posture of a square with his feet. It has also been related to what the Greeks called *Gnomon*, a square of two unequal limbs or arms, the usual ratio being 3:4, and it is even suggested that the sacred symbol found in the centre of the Lodge is really the initial letter of this word. Accordingly, W. Meeson asserts:

> 'He that is truly square, well polished and uprightly fixed is well qualified and fit to be a member of the most honourable society that ever existed — Freemasonry.'
>
> 'He that hath such a one with any possible engagement is freed from all trouble and anxiety about the performance of it. For his words are the breathing of his heart, he promiseth and is faithful to his trust and is an utter stranger to things of a double meaning. As he endeavoreth at all times to give satisfaction to others, so he is sure as a reward to his constancy to be admitted a member of that most amiable society where every member is perfectly square, perfectly polished and perfectly upright.'

The square, if well applied, will show where the gavel and chisel should be applied if need be, and how far necessary. In the same manner it was even asserted by Aristotle that he who bears the shocks of fortune valiantly is truly good and of square posture without reproof. Now he that would smooth himself into such a perfect square should often try himself by the perfect square of justice and equity. For thou shalt love the Lord thy God with all thy heart, with all thy mind, with all thy soul, with all thy strength, and they neighbour as thyself, by doing to all men as we would they should do to us. Brotherly love, relief and truth.

The view is expressed by J. S. M. Ward:

> 'In general the square represents matter, but at the same time we should bear in mind that as symbolising the letter G it also stands for God. This appears to be contradictory but in reality it is not, since matter is also Divine and like the Spirit indestructible as modern scientists know. Matter may change its form a hundred times, but it is not thereby destroyed, and we may truly say that matter is only one form of the outward manifestation of God in His Creation. The square therefore teaches us that God created matter out of His own substance, and this being so it is also Divine and Eternal though transient in form.'

With all due respect to J. S. M. Ward, there is a basic fallacy in the structure of his moralizing in this regard. Spirit is eternal and not divine, and matter being the manifestation of His Creation, even though indestructible, cannot be divine. There is a difference between eternity and divinity, and the Creator and the created cannot be divine at the same time. Indestructibility does not constitute divinity. That being so, a symbol that represents matter cannot represents God. The analogy of a painter or a playwright with his works would appear to be apt here. No matter how expressive of the nature of the artist, a painting *per se* cannot be the artist.

The square is also accepted by masons symbolically as representing justice. Indeed, in ancient Egypt, the gods were depicted as sitting on squares on their thrones, when acting as judges. It is significant that the JW requests in this degree that he be proved by the square. The alert masonic mind ought to be tempted to ask why, if he does not already know.

If the centre point of a standard lodge layout is taken, using it as the centre, *ie* the position occupied by the FC, and an arc of a circle is described with a radius equal to half the length of the lodge, *ie* the distance either to the RWM's or the SW's pedestal, the arc on the south side should properly pass through the JW's pedestal. Accordingly, the two lines drawn from the end of a diameter of the circle, say from the RWM's or SW's pedestal to meet at any point on the circumference of that circle, say the JW's pedestal, the angle contained by those two lines is 90°, a right or square angle. This makes the true layout of the lodge as set by the positions of the principal officers into a right-angled triangle, with the JW sitting at the right angle — Colin Dyer (*Symbolism in Craft Masonry*, Lewis Masonic).

Who then is better qualified than the JW to request that he be proved by the square? In this moralizing and accepting the positions of the wardens in the south and west, the candidate as a craftsman in this degree is shown at the mid point. In his progress through the lodge squaring from west to east, he has reached the centre of the lodge, half way between the SW and the RMW where in former times the letter G was displayed in a pentangle on the chequered floor. It is therefore considered a restful degree, one of peace and tranquillity, with some sense of achievement.

Thus we find that the square in itself is said to represent God, the matter or the lower nature of man which is a manifestation of God. It likewise stands for His essential attribute of justice, which is His will, and hence a test of right conduct.

The 1° represents the rough ashlar which has to be worked by the square. His spiritual nature is symbolized by an ear of corn near a fall of water, a stone to be used in the building of the Jerusalem above out of perfected stones (spirits) whose passage through the winding staircase even to the throne of God must be guided by the square in faith, hope and charity.

3

A SPRIG OF ACACIA — SYMBOLIC SIGNIFICANCE

Conducted through the intricate windings of this mortal life, we are prepared by contemplation for the closing hours of our existence as our inevitable destiny while the acacia or evergreen is an emblem of our faith in the immortal part within us that shall survive the grave.

It is accepted in the philosophy of Freemasonry that the mysteries of the Order cannot be revealed to the full view of the seeker unless he achieves by positive striving a clear understanding and realisation of the inner meanings of both the symbols and ceremonial drama involved. It is a science in which every character, figure and emblem depicted in the lodges has a moral tendency and serves to inculcate the practice of virtue and ennoble the lives of all its genuine professors. It is for this reason that the science is described as a peculiar system of morality veiled in allegory and illustrated by symbols. It is for this reason that the craftsman is admonished that the study of our science and more especially its hidden or symbolic meaning is not only a valuable branch of education tending to polish and adorn the mind, but being of a divine and moral nature is enriched with the most useful and inspiring knowledge. It is for this reason that the Mason is exhorted to bend with humility and resignation to the will of TGAOTU and to dedicate his heart thus purified from every baneful and malignant passion, fitted only for the reception of truth and wisdom.

Among the symbols that adorn not only the temples and ceremonials, but also masonic regalias as a constant reminder of its significance, is the *Sprig of Acacia*. In its passive quietness we tend to underestimate its significance, and it is for this reason that I am attracted to produce this chapter for the benefit of all, and more particularly those who may tend not to recognize the full import of its adoption into the rituals and ceremonials of the Craft.

Since Masonry is described as a progressive science, the search for the truth — 'the sacred symbol that was lost' — will continue until each individual mason attains sufficient inner awareness to enable him to live his life knowingly in his attempt to ascend Jacob's ladder, whose base is anchored on the VSL and whose summit extends to the ethereal mansions, veiled from mortal eyes by the starry firmament, and even to the throne of God.

History and Mythical Appearance

(a) The acacia is an important symbol in Masonry but does not appear in the ceremonies until the 3° though it is a symbol that is seen every day in the masonic lodges. It is regarded for most of the time by the uninitiated as an ordinary decorative design for the superficial or more aesthetic enrichment of the masonic regalia.

To the initiated however, it means more, even without a further search into its mythical and historical origins. It is because this knowledge might assist the newly initiated in his daily quest for understanding that I have found it necessary to include it in this volume.

Botanically it is the *acacia vera* of Tournefort (*fig 2B*) and the *mimosa nilotica* of Linnoeus (*fig 2A*) called Babul tree in India. Its contribution to the welfare of mankind generally is that it is the tree from which gum arabic is produced and it is known to have grown abundantly in the vicinity of Jerusalem. Although there had been some controversy as to whether such trees could grow as far north as Jerusalem, it has been settled on the testimonies of Lt Lynch and Rabbi Joseph Swarz that several varieties did grow in Palestine.

It also occurs in the VSL where it is called *shittim* the plural of *shitta* (*Isaiah* XLI).

It is an established fact that in most ancient mystical or religious orders initiations had been related to some plant peculiar to each, which occupied an important position in the ceremonials and which was consecrated by its own esoteric meaning and by constant and prominent use in the ceremonial rites became adopted as the symbol of that initiation or rite.

The significance of this however, is not merely the adoption as a symbol but the sacredness with which the plant is regarded and the lessons deduced therefrom. Thus the lettuce (*fig 2E*) was the sacred plant in the mysteries of Adonis and it assumed the place of the acacia. Similarly, the *akoko* leaf assumed (*fig 2F*) the position of sacredness in the ancient mysteries of initiation and installation in

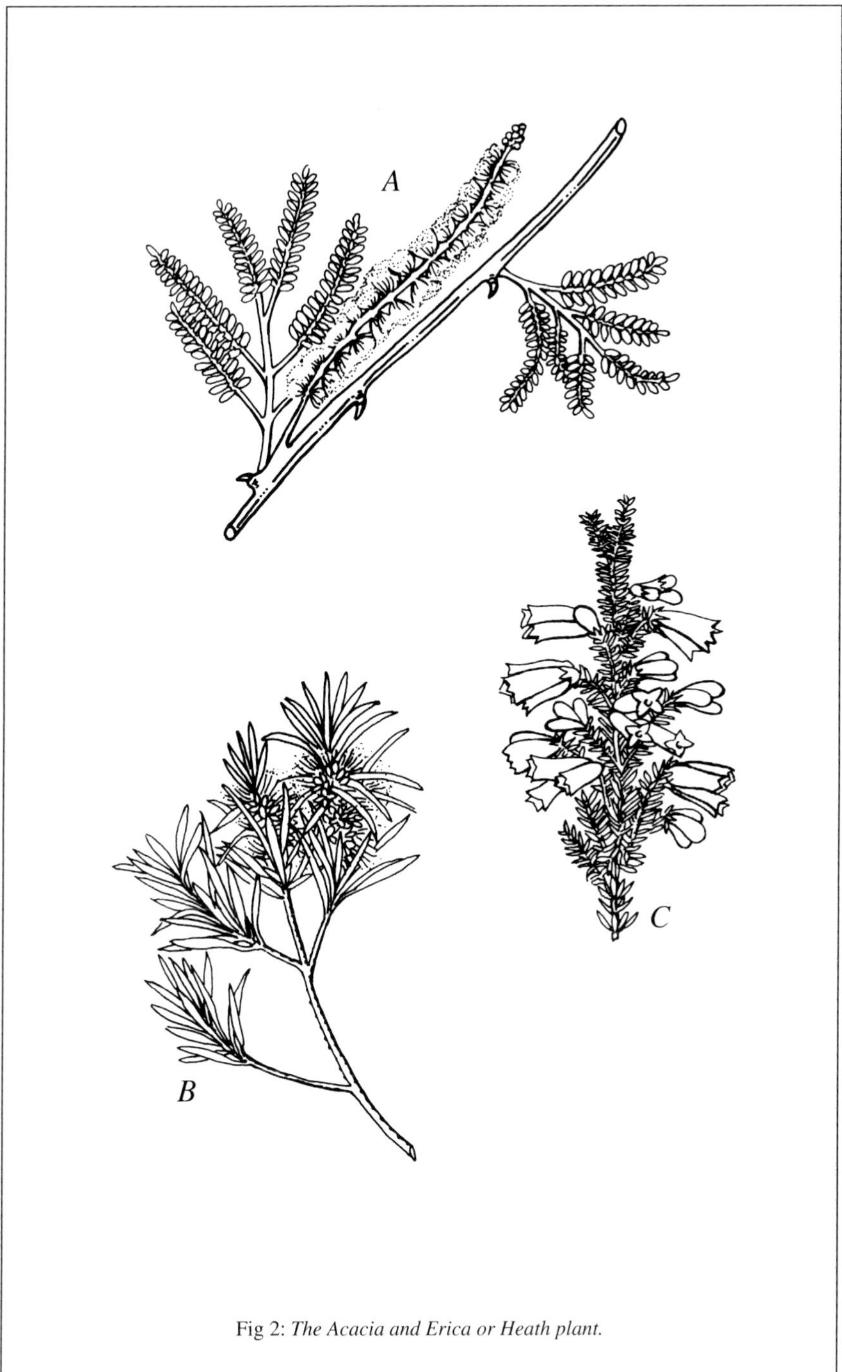

Fig 2: *The Acacia and Erica or Heath plant.*

Fig 2: *Lotus, Lettuce, Akoko & Mistletoe plants.*

Oduduwaland, in Nigeria. The Brahmatical rites of India adopted the lotus (*fig 2D*) as the sacred plant and it was subsequently adopted by the Egyptians.

The Ijaws and the Igbos in Nigeria adopted the *emulu* (palm shoot — *fig 3*) as the sacred symbol not only in their mystery orders as emblematically representative of hallowed shrines, but also as a sign of immortality at funerals, deriving from popular belief that the symbolic plant would protect the living from the evil effects of the immortal soul of the dead. In the same manner the mythical plant among the ancient Druids was the mistletoe while the (*fig 2G*) Egyptians revered the erica or heath (*fig 2C*). Among the Greeks the myrtle was regarded with the same symbolism and sacredness in their mystery orders. Other examples abound in other ancient mystery or religious orders, most of which are uncodified. Those professing such orders were known to have had a higher spiritual perception than is dreamed of by modern man who is governed by the intellect, which renders even his relationship with his animistic guides weak and indolent.

It is recognised as a common phenomenon that in all these mystery or religious orders, while the sacred plant is a symbol of initiation, the initiation itself is symbolic of resurrection or transfiguration into a new spiritual and future life, a death to the old self and a rebirth into a new life which recognizes the immortality of the soul.

From this point of view, if Masonry is taken to replace the ancient mystery orders, the acacia is equally taken to replace the lotus, mistletoe, *akoko*, erica and *emulu* as a symbol of initiation teaching the lesson of rebirth into a new life. However, while the ancient mystery orders accepted initiation as the stage of rebirth, Masonry accepts this rebirth at the 3° while initiation is regarded as preparation of the mind for the reception of truth. The lessons however are the same, but the mode and stage of imparting them may be different.

The Sacred Attributes

The acacia appears in the Volume of the Sacred Law as *shittim*, in *Isaiah* XLI. Very significantly, it had always been singled out from among the other trees in the forest by the sacred purpose to which it has pleased God to devote it through the inspiration of His messengers.

The Holy Writ bears testimony to the fact that through inspiration Moses was ordered by the GAOTU to construct the Ark of the covenant from the shittim tree, together with the staves with which the Ark was to be borne. Equally, he was ordered to make the table for the shewbread in shittim. He was also ordered to make the altar and the other sacred furniture in the tabernacle in shittim. Above all, it was his instruction to construct the Tabernacle and its interior boards in shittim. The acacia was therefore an esteemed wood among the Hebrews, and Isaiah in recounting the promises of God's mercy to the Israelites on their return from captivity tells them that among other things for their relief and refreshment in the wilderness, he will plant the acacia. To the Jews therefore the wood from which the sanctuary of the tabernacle and the Holy Ark had been constructed must of necessity be regarded as more sacred than any other tree.

In view of the importance that Masonry attaches to the sacred truth of the immortality of the soul, the early Masons appropriated this hallowed plant to the equally sacred purpose of a symbol in the ceremonial of the immortality of the soul.

The Symbolic Relations of the Acacia in Freemasonry

In general, the acacia would appear to have three main symbolic relations in Freemasonry in its philosophical concepts:

A symbol of the immortality of the soul

The acacia in mythical Freemasonry is essentially a symbol of the immortality of the soul, that great and final lesson that we are taught to learn, after having been conducted through the intricate windings of this mortal life by pure contemplation of the spiritual or hidden mysteries of the science. In essence this stage is a discovery of ourselves in creation, an awareness of our spiritual nature regarding which the RWM gives a lead in the 3° when he requests of his wardens 'Whence came you?' and 'Whither are your directing your course?'. 'That which was lost' the mason hopes to find with the centre, the point from which he cannot err, and that point is the spirit. It follows therefore that the reference to the immortality of the soul relates to its core which is the spirit, for the soul, being itself ethereal, must detach from the spirit in immortality, just as the body, being gross material, must detach from the soul at death. This is the important doctrine which it is the great design of Freemasonry to teach and which may be understood only by masons who by contemplation have opened their minds to the reception of truth and wisdom.

Even though we have been prepared by contemplation for the closing hours of our existence, our inevitable destiny, we are still reminded in the impressive funeral rites of our Order that the evergreen is the emblem of our faith in the immortality of the soul. By this we are reminded that we have an immortal part within us which shall survive the grave and to listen to the voice of nature which bears

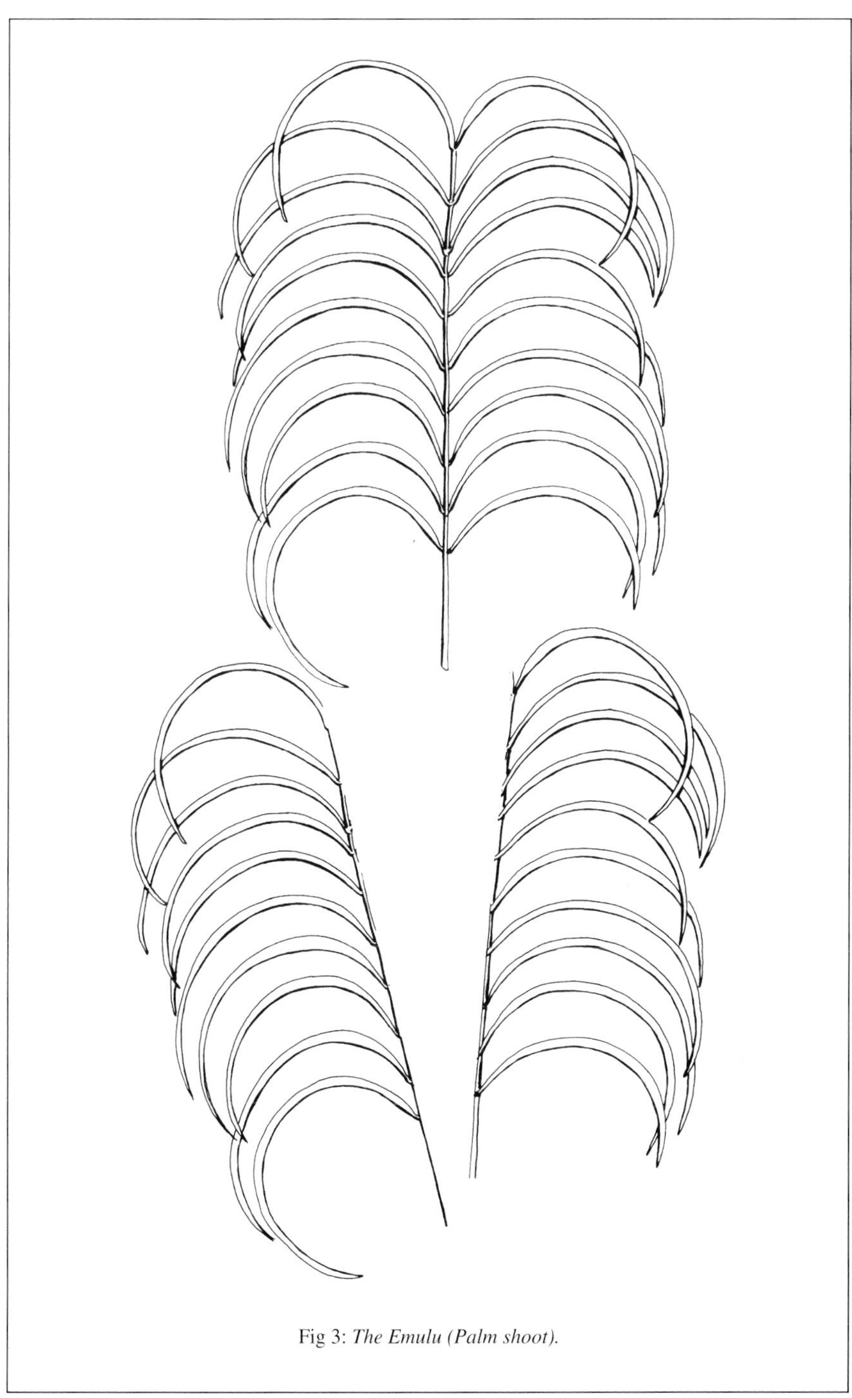

Fig 3: *The Emulu (Palm shoot).*

witness that even in this perishable frame resides a vital and immortal principle. That principle again relates to that which was lost, which the mason hopes to find with the centre.

In ancient custom, not altogether abandoned even now, mourners at a funeral would carry a sprig of some evergreen in their hands, or even bedeck vehicles with some evergreen. In some cases the evergreen is deposited in the grave. The carrying and bedecking of coffins with the palm shoot is common among the Igbos, Ogbias and Ijaws in Nigeria, while the cedar and cypress were common among the Jews. The Hebrews on the other hand were known to plant a sprig of acacia at the head of the grave of a departed friend, while the Greeks had the custom of bedecking tombs with flowers and herbs, particularly the amaranth and myrtle. Significantly, amaranth is 'never fading' and seems therefore to indicate the true symbolic meaning of its usage. The ancients believed that the acacia is incorruptible and not liable to destruction from the attacks of insects or animals, thus also symbolizing the incorruptible nature of the soul being an emanation from TGAOTU. The emphasis that Masons place on the sprig of acacia as an emblem of immortality, whose principal lesson is a realisation of our inevitable destiny, can thus be better understood.

A Symbol of Initiation

The acacia as a symbol of initiation has been considered by some writers to be the most interesting of all the philosophical interpretations and also the primary and original, all others being secondary and incidental. This view is correct when related to initiations into the ancient mystery and religious orders, since initiation into the Order was considered to be the final revelation of the mysteries. In Freemasonry the term Initiation referred to here is an introduction to the awareness of the reward of immortality after this transitory life has passed away. This stage is reached only in the 3°, as the Initiation in the 1° refers to the entry of man into his mortal existence, and the acceptance of light to enlighten his mind for the reception of truth and wisdom guided by faith in the VSL and conduct regulated by the square. It is the strict adherence to these principles that leads the mason to the awakening of the inner spiritual initiation, the most valuable tenents of which are symbolically comprehended between the points of the compasses and the reward of immortality symbolically represented by the sprig of acacia.

It is for the reason that this lesson is so vital that the sprig is worn on our regalia as a constant physical reminder to all true and worthy masons.

A symbol of innocence

Apart from the ordinary meaning of acacia as a particular plant, the Greek language has a second meaning which refers to the innocence and purity of life. From this is derived a secondary symbolic meaning of the acacia denoting innocence. The planting of the acacia on each solitary grave refers to one whose virtuous conduct, integrity of life and fidelity to his trusts have been presented as patterns to the Craft.

Conclusion

We thus find that the acacia in masonic terms portrays three symbolic but significant meanings: it is a symbol of immortality, of initiation and of innocence.

4

SIGNIFICANCE OF MASONIC INITIATION

That our minds may open up for the understanding of the symbolism of the esoteric nature of our science we are initiated and allowed to perceive that our level of contemplation and awakening is a factor of individual inner endeavour and experience.

Introduction

THE FOUNDATION ON which Freemasonry rests is described as the practice of every moral and social virtue regulating the actions of its professors by the divine precepts contained in the Volume of the Sacred Law. In Masonry these principles are illustrated in the allegory of the building of a temple, King Solomon's Temple, the principal materials being stones, and the principal artisans being masons.

The allegory of temple building in Masonry refers to the building of a spiritual temple and masonic Initiation is the beginning of the preparation of the materials for the temple. The stone taken directly from the quarry and represented in physical and symbolic terms by the rough ashlar can only refer to the unpolished personality of the initiate guided through the processes in the system to the perfect ashlar fit for the building of the spiritual temple not made with hands eternal in the heavens.

Because the science is esoteric, it is capable of appreciation and understanding at different levels by members even of the same degree within the Craft, not because such knowledge is withheld from some but because the level of contemplation and awakening is a factor of individual inner endeavour and experiencing.

Initiation therefore is an opening up of the mind to the understanding of the symbolism of the esoteric nature of our science. It is therefore the degree of enlightenment that comes from such experiencing rather than any intellectual or academic knowledge or the grandeur of the ceremonial rites that constitutes true initiation.

The Ancient Mysteries and Masonry

All the ancient mysteries, including the great uncoded African ancient mysteries, had a form of initiation regarded as an emblem of admission into participation in secret worship of a deity to which none were admitted other than those who had been selected at preparatory ceremonies of initiation. It is this secret worship that was termed the mysteries known to the initiates alone who were admitted only after long and painful trials and probations, the revelation of which was believed to be more than their life was worth.

The ceremonies were generally funereal in character, celebrating in symbolic terms the death and resurrection of some cherished being with either an heroic esteem or godly devotion. Candidates were subjected to probations and rituals varying in character and degree in rites practiced in the darkness of night, in forest, subterranean cavern, or heights and cliffs of mountains and rocks. These mysteries undoubtedly owed their origin to the desire to establish an esoteric philosophy whose sublime truths could be entrusted only to those who had been prepared to receive them. The confinement of these doctrines to a system of secret knowledge guarded by most rigid rites was considered the only way to protect them from profanation, corruption, undesired innovation and superstition existing in the world around. The prevention of intrusion and the preservation of these sublime truths was the original object of initiation, together with the adoption of a convenient means whereby the initiated was known to the exclusion of the uninitiated.

The Abbe Rabon in a learned work on the subject (Paris, 1870) places the origin of initiation at that remote period when crime had just begun its growth on earth and the virtuous in earnest desire to avoid contagion retired into solitude to devote themselves to a life of contemplation and cultivation of the useful sciences. These recluse students, having gained much inner knowledge of creation through contemplation, inverted certain signs to remind people of the times of their festivals, labour, etc. This was the origin of the symbols and hieroglyphics in use among priests of many nations. Having thus become guides and leaders of moral conduct, these sages set up strict courses of trials and examinations to enable them to select men qualified to participate in their learning and labours. This, according to the author, was the origin of initiations in antiquity. Accordingly, the

Magi, Brahmans, Gymnosophists, Druids, Essenes, and Egyptian priests lived in sequestered habitations and caverns to achieve this purpose which led to discoveries in astronomy, mathematics, chemistry etc based on the purity of their morals and an understanding of the laws of nature.

Through this discovery and understanding, the true object of the mysteries became the teaching of the doctrine of the unity of God as opposed to the polytheistic notions then existing, and in connection with this the doctrine of a future happier life for the initiate after this mortal existence. Accordingly, Isocrates declared 'Those who have been initiated into the mysteries entertain better hopes both as to the end of life and the whole of futurity'.

Much testimony as to the esoteric character of the mysteries has been given by other ancients including Plutarch and Cicero. Plutarch says, 'All the mysteries refer to a future life and the state of the soul after death'. He further states 'We have been instructed in the religious rites of Dionysus that the soul is immortal and that there is a future state of existence'. And Cicero tells us that in the mysteries of Ceres at Eleusis the initiated were taught to live happily and to die 'in the hope of a blessed futurity'.

The ceremonies conducted in the solemnity of night in strange but pleasant surroundings coupled with songs and dances with all the resources of art, sensual beauty and serenity are calculated to take a firm grip on the imagination while exciting in the participant conflicting sentiments of terror and calm, sorrow and fear, hope and reflective observation and perhaps even a resigned credulity. Even among initiates, the esoteric character of the mysteries was preserved by the most powerful sanctions. An oath of secrecy was usually administered in the most solemn form to the initiate, violation of which was considered a sacrilegious crime, punishable even by death.

Masonic Initiation

The term Initiation was used by the Romans to designate admission to the mysteries of their sacred and secret rites. It is derived from *initia* signifying the first principles of a science. Thus Justin (*Lib* XI C7) says in Midas, King of the Phrygians that he was initiated into the mysteries of Orpheus. From the Latins the masons adopted the word to signify reception into their order.

The initiate is also called 'Entered Apprentice' in a fairly universal way among Freemasons, in French *l'apprentice*, in Spanish *aprendiz*, Italian *apprendente* and in German *Lehrling*, all of which mean 'learner'.

Plate C: *Bro David Liddell-Grainger of Ayton.*

To be a fit and proper person for admission as a mason, the candidate must be a free man, of mature age, sound judgement and strict morals. He must believe in the Supreme Ruler of the universe and so declare. He must also declare his trust in TGAOTU, in all cases of difficulty and danger, and declare his preparedness to render himself more extensively serviceable to his fellow creatures, while his actions are kept in due bounds with all mankind.

These declarations and assurances of attainment, coupled with his acknowledged social status, would tend conclusively to make the candidate already perfectly respectable and acceptable in the society in which he lives. What else does he therefore desire by seeking for initiation into the Order, other than an inner awareness of an urge for a greater understanding of his place in creation that is shielded from his mortal eyes and beyond the ordinary five senses that govern our physical lives, a greater bestirring of his inner core for spiritual uplift in joyous exultation to TGAOTU.

The candidate is described as being poor and in a state of darkness, of good report but must be well and worthily recommended and approved in open Lodge to be entitled to participation in the mysteries and privileges. He declares he is uninfluenced by mercenary or other unworthy motive. However, it is stimulating to note that, despite the confidence implicit in these declarations and assurances, the candidate expresses two significant desires: that he is prompted to solicit the privileges from a *general desire* for knowledge; and that he *desires LIGHT* after having been kept for some time in a state of darkness. It is here significant that the restoration to light as well as the quest for knowledge come from a desire of the candidate.

There can be no inward stirring of the spirit without desire. For this reason spiritual advance is dependent on personal endeavour but the candidate is admonished to rely on the VSL to guide his faith; his actions must be regulated by the square and his passions kept in due bounds with all mankind, as it is only through constant practice of these that we are enabled to vibrate in that purity of life and action which will at all times distinguish us as freemasons.

Does Masonry as practised today create an atmosphere and circumstance for the fulfilment of this desire in the initiate?

Is the initiate after his admission not left with mere illusion as to what the Craft is in relation to his expectations, social and spiritual?

The Illusions

To be able to appraise usefully whatever answers are provided to these postulates, it should be remembered at all times that accession

Plate D: *Chief Oluyinka Olumide, Hon JGW, Past District Grand Master.*

to inner spiritual knowledge through enlightenment is a factor of individual inner endeavour and experience which is beyond communication by any of our senses. Preparedness of the mind for its reception is not dependent on academic or intellectual ability, but it is significant to observe that where these principles are meant to be understood with the aid of symbols, then no real understanding of the principles can be achieved without an understanding of the symbols and an ability to lift the veil of symbolism. In the absence of these capabilities, the symbols become confused with the doctrine or philosophy they represent which is illusory.

The ancient mysteries developed from a system of purely secret worship to the gaining of inner knowledge and spiritual awakening and thence to the invention of symbols and signs for the protection of such knowledge. The professors then developed into guides and leaders of moral conduct, enforcing strict courses of trials and examinations to select men qualified to participate. This was the origin of initiation in antiquity, the true object of which then became the teaching of the unity of God, the associated moral truths and the prospect of futurity after this transitory existence.

We know that the main object of Craft Masonry is to seek for that which was lost which we hope to find with the centre, and that the loss was due to the fall of man, symbolically and allegorically illustrated as the untimely death of our master. We also know that in the process we seek to find the answers to the questions 'What am I?', 'Whence came I?' and 'Whither go I?' and that we shall be guided in the process by the principles of moral truths and justice. We also know that it is for the purpose of achieving these objectives and protecting these sublime principles from profanation that masonic Initiations are held.

Every candidate who has gone through the ceremony of masonic Initiation will confess that no experience in his existence has created so lasting an impression. His application for proposal had been preceded by great uncertainty. The communication of his success at the ballot had filled his heart with confidence and hope that already had found a base in his prerequisite qualifications, and his answers to the questions at the interview, which may take place. The formality of the dress mode communicated to him added more confidence and grandeur, causing his whole being to anticipate the night of his Initiation with great expectation. At this stage none of these feelings would appear to be of a spiritual nature, as sheer excitement and sensuality seem to be controlling his being. His expectations suddenly reach an anticlimax in the mode of his preparation in the room adjoining the lodge, when he has to submit to the humble but firm instructions of Bro Tyler who has taken control of him in his sudden solitude. At this stage there is an interchange of sentiments of humility and humiliation which is broken with sentiments of hope from the faint sound of the opening ode that filters through the Temple. This hope is suddenly replaced with extreme fear and uncertainty with the introduction of the cable tow and hoodwink, shortly followed by the rather strange knock signalling the candidate humbly soliciting for admission into the mysteries and privileges. From that moment to the restoration of material light, his feeling is one of complete resignation, childlike humility and inspired credulity. This is strengthened by the unique setting of the lodge and the force of the lectures.

Thus in one evening the candidate is led through a peculiar system which takes control of the imagination of the heart, inspiring within him sentiments alternating and conflicting in uncertainty and hope, terror and calm, fear and resignation, felicitation and reflective observation, humility and resigned credulity, so that the mind is fully prepared for the reception of truth and wisdom and he looks upon the lodge and its members with great expectation and hope for guidance. Very often this is illusory, as the initiate soon realises that the lives of some of his senior brethren are anything but exemplary, that he cannot receive satisfactory explanations even on issues as basic as the symbols found in the lodge, that he is unable to gain access to libraries that may assist his research, that preference and recognition are given to parrot-like repetition of the rituals rather than a true understanding of their symbolic import.

Consequently the path towards his inner re-awakening is made so difficult that even the removal of the hoodwink leaves him a blind man groping along his masonic path unable to see the splendours around him. He stands before the great works of creation like a drunkard or a sick man.

Further Symbolism of Initiation

It is recognized that the first degree in the masonic system is concerned with the principles of moral justice and truth, its object being to purify the heart from every baneful and malignant passion. There are other symbolic meanings to which initiation in the first degree relates. The 'entered apprentice' degree symbolizes the creation of man and his first perception of light. Perception of light in this regard has two concepts, the introduction of the soul and the spirit core in the human cloak, and the experience of physical light at birth.

Masonry having its reliance on the TGAOTU does not get involved in any controversies in cosmogony. In the form of creation as contained in the Volume of the Sacred Law we read 'And God said, Let us make man in our own image, after our likeness: and let him have domination over the fish of the sea, and over the fowl of the air, and over the cattle, and over all the earth, and over every creeping thing that creepeth on the earth' (*Gen* I.26, 27). So God created man in His own image. It is further stated in the Holy Writ: 'And the Lord God formed man of the dust of the ground, and *breathed into his nostrils the breath of life, and man became a living soul*' (*Gen* 2:7). Similarly, various other speculative theories of the origin and creation of man and his spontaneous generation exist with other religions whose protagonists may or may not be masons.

They also exist in other ancient mystery orders in different forms, but with the same basic belief in the origin of life as anchored in the introduction of the soul or light, which is the animating force. Accordingly, from the Egyptians: 'the fertilising mud left by the Nile and exposed to the vivifying action of heat induced by the sun's rays brought forth germs which sprang up as the bodies of men'. The Mandans, a tribe in north America, relate that the great spirit moulded two figures of clay which he dried and animated with the breath of his mouth, one receiving the name of First man and the other Companion. The god of Tahiti, Taeroa, is said to have formed man of the red earth according to the inhabitants. Similarly, in Peru the first man created by the Divine Omnipotence is called *Alpa Camasra*, or animated earth. The Chaldeans call Adam the man whom the earth produced, who lay without movement, without life and without breath, until his soul had been given him.

Without wishing to go into more illustrations, the significant observation here is that the life of man in creation begins only after animation by the Creator and in most cases through the breath of the Creator or injection of the soul which forms the cloak in which the spirit resides as the core of man. It is the awareness of this core that masonic science seeks to awaken in the inner consciousness of its professors, and masonic Initiation is an introduction to and preparation for the path towards this awareness.

The Interconnecting Relationships

There are marked resemblances between the ceremonies of the ancient mysteries and masonic rite in content and philosophy if not in form. As to their relationship or implied connections, five principal theories exist, most of which deal with the supposed chain of descent from the ancient mysteries to Freemasonry. For our purposes the truest and most acceptable theory would appear to be that which attributes any resemblances to accidents of human thought, guided by the purity

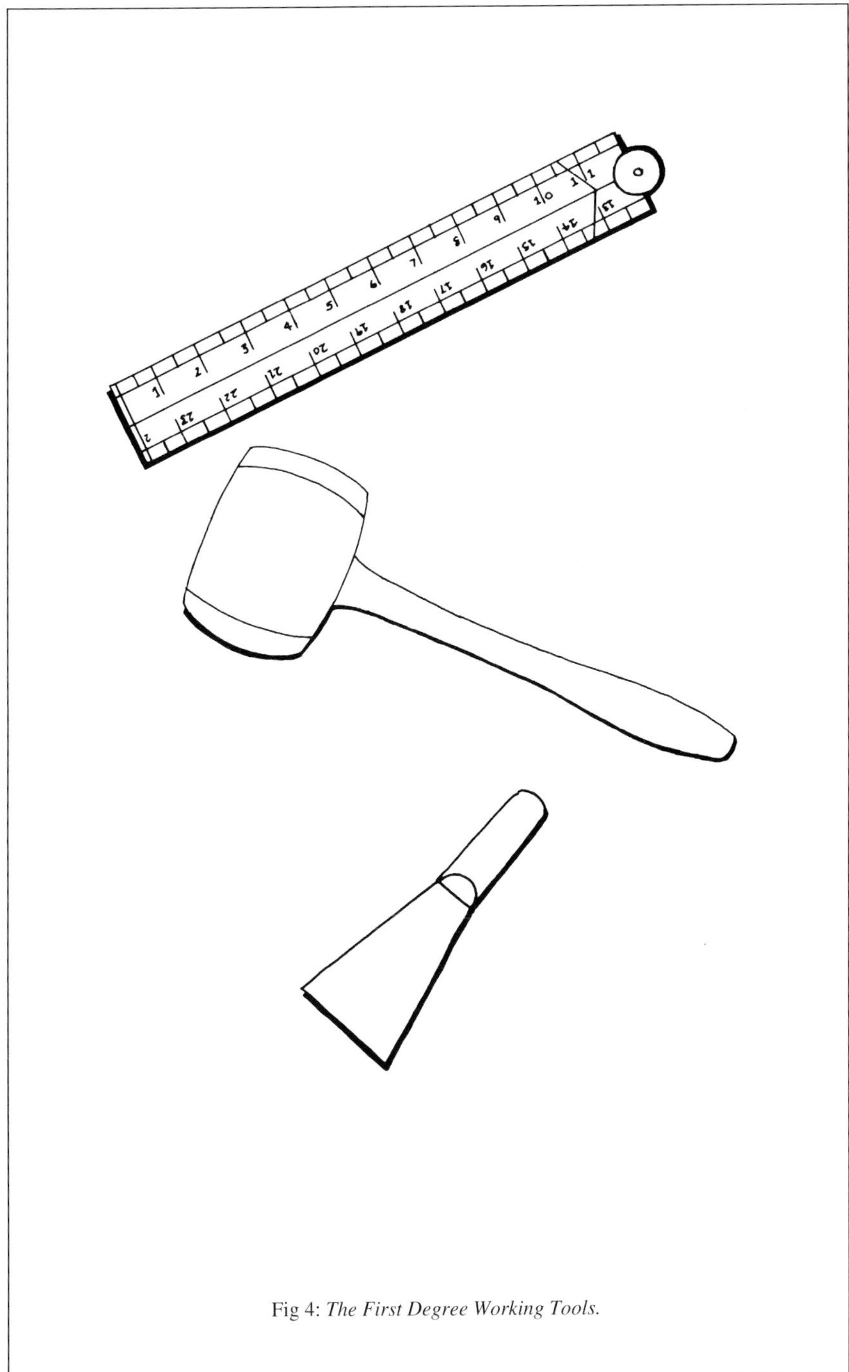

Fig 4: *The First Degree Working Tools.*

their lives through inspiration to a consciousness of the truth which is eternal and universal and which transcends time and space. The basic lesson is to teach the reality of the futurity of life by understanding its origin and in this the legends of the 3° in Masonry are fairly identical with the legends of the Eleusinian, the Dionysian, the Cabiric and the Adonic mystery ceremonies. Although these mystery orders continued long after the era of Christianity, they degenerated subsequently because they threw open their gates to initiates without sufficient scrutiny of the candidates' past life and without demanding proof of irreproachable character and conduct. *If you have a good Lodge, be careful to keep it select.* These orders failed to keep access to the secrets select.

In the candidate's path towards his daily progress in masonic knowledge, the significance of the working tools presented in the 1° — the 24 inch gauge, the mallet, and the chisel — indicate the duties and the mode of performance required of the initiate in his spiritual path. These are supposed to be fully assimilated into his being in his daily practical life.

Masonry acknowledges that man has inner qualities inherent in the 'sphere of instincts' which sometimes regulate his behaviour particularly when the spirit is indolent. Through this instinctive behaviour he expresses his emotions in the experiencing of desire and aversion, pleasure and sorrow, attraction and repulsion. His appetites and passions are exercised according to his values of good and evil, morally expressed in accordance with social standards. Masonic Initiation in acknowledging these qualities cautions their exercise and expression with sufficient prudence to open the mind for the reception of greater truths which lie at the threshold of the second degree which coincides with the world of reason and intellectual standards, whence the candidate is prepared for his inner awakening into spiritual knowledge which is supreme and transcends the limitations of intellect and reason. 'It is for this reason that the candidate is admonished: "You are now permitted to extend your researches into the more hidden mysteries of our science".'

The three degrees in Masonry would therefore tend to reflect this basic human structure, and without achieving the three inwardly we cannot be the perfect ashlars fit for the Spiritual Temple. The three degrees reflect three subjective worlds — the moral, intellectual and spiritual. Masonry would therefore appear to be the philosophical reconstruction of the creation of man and his journey through life, initiation being the beginning. When our minds are sufficiently conditioned, we come to the inevitable conclusion that even the greater though emblematical lights in Freemasonry are still merely symbolically representative of the true light which can only be perceived, the original light which came into being with the great fiat *Let there be Light*. That light came into being when the physical lights of the sun that rules the day and the moon that governs the night were yet to be created by *TGAOTU*. 'What therefore was that Light?'

5

LIGHT THAT IS BUT DARKNESS VISIBLE

Let your light so shine before men that they may see your works and glorify God. Matt. 5.16

THE CONCEPT OF light or the word itself has always, from time immemorial, occupied a dominant position in the philosophies of all ancient religions and mystery orders. In ordinary parlance the word is given several definitions which on reflection tend to lead to a realisation of deeper meanings which have adorned the philosophies of ancient mystery orders, including Freemasonry.

Some of the most common definitions are as follows:

(a) The natural agent that stimulates sight and makes things visible. This would presuppose that the object can physically exist and yet not be visible to a person whose sight is not sufficiently stimulated (as would be the case with a blind man, or a man whose sight is failing). Sight could of course be physical or spiritual.

(b) It is also defined as the amount of illumination in a place or a person's share of it. This also presupposes that no matter the amount of illumination, it is only each person's share that constitutes light to him, for he who is not privileged to receive a share would be in darkness even in the midst of such illumination.

(c) It is also described as the object from which light emanates such as the sun, a lamp, a candle, fire, a lighthouse, etc. This limits the definition to the material object itself as against the concept.

(d) It is also defined as the quality of brightening with animation. The introduction here of the concept of animation leads us to the principles of disintegration and integration, forming and reforming, dissolution and reconstruction which constitutes the core of the basic theories of creation.

All these definitions relate to sight which is the faculty of seeing by response of the brain to the action of light on the eyes in all things that relate to the gross material world limited to time and space in accordance with the capacity of the brain which governs the intellect.

The Concept of Light in Ancient Religions and Mystery Orders

In all ancient philosophies man has always contended with the doctrine of the two antagonistic principles of light and darkness, wisdom and ignorance, good and evil. Indeed there is hardly any ancient system that did not possess the basic recognition of light with reverence as being emblematically representative of the eternal principles of goodness and wisdom as against evil and ignorance. These ancient systems of religion and esoteric science went further to exhibit prominently an emblematic relation between material light and mental illumination, primordial knowledge or the ever active primordial energy. Accordingly the Jewish Kabalistic doctrine states that all space was filled with infinite intellectual light before the creation of the world, that future worlds were created by emanation from the infinite intellectual light, and eventually that man was also created by subsequent emanations. These principles of regarding light as emblematical of deeper meanings were common among the Egyptians and the Persians as enunciated by the dogma of Zoroaster and the Brahmans as illustrated in their Holy Writ the Bhagavat Geeta.

It is a reflection of these doctrines that leads us also to a conscious contemplation of the true meaning of the great fiat *Let there be light, and there was light.* It is significant to note that even man in his material existence in reacting to his own surroundings is filled with sentiments of fear when he is face to face with darkness while his reaction to light is that of joy and happiness.

Masonic Concept of Light

All masons know or ought to know that 'light' is one of the cardinal words that form the main fabric of Speculative Masonry. It is not only the first symbol that is ceremonially introduced to the initiate, but continues all through his progress in Freemasonry. Truth and wisdom constitute part of light which pervades the whole basis of Freemasonry to the extent that Masons are even called the Sons of Light.

In the 1° alone the word is introduced to the candidate in three different perspectives, *viz* the material light, or the lesser light, the emblematical light or the greater light, and the spiritual light or the creative will of the TGAOTU.

These concepts and others that follow after the 1° are amply enshrouded in illuminating phraseology remembered by every Freemason. Their full import may not be perceived by all but they are constantly reminded in the rituals during ceremonies in the following manner:

(a) 'Having been kept for some time in a state of darkness, what in your present situation do you most desire?' — 'LIGHT' (Masonic Rituals 1°).

(b) 'Having been restored to the blessing of material light, let me now direct your attention to what we consider the three great though emblematical lights in freemasonry' (Masonic Rituals 1°).

(c) 'Let me now beg you to observe that the light of a Master Mason is but darkness visible' (Masonic Rituals 3°).

There are other references to light that are still worthy of note. 'To bring to light' or 'to see the light' means 'initiation' technically. The old rituals of the last century postulated furnishing of lodge rooms with three windows — east, west and south — known as 'fixed lights' to light the men to, at and from work.

From the foregoing it is obvious that to the mason light has a deeper meaning which is darkness to the uninitiated or even the rough ashlar mason, but visible to the worthy Mason and to the worthy mason only. *What therefore is this light that is Darkness visible?*

The Light That is Darkness Visible

The first and most important qualification for becoming a mason is 'belief in a SUPREME BEING'. From this belief arises a second belief that all things were made at the creative fiat of THE MOST HIGH. This belief is clearly illustrated in the prayer at the raising of any candidate to the sublime degree of Master Mason — *Almighty and Eternal God, Architect and Ruler of the Universe, at whose creative fiat all things first were made*. (Masonic Rituals 3°.)

What therefore is the creative fiat at which all things first were made? The VSL bears testimony that in the beginning God created Heaven and earth, and the earth was without form and void (*Gen* 1:1, 2). Then came the great fiat, *And God said, Let there be light, and there was light* and God saw the light and it was good, and God divided the light from the darkness and God called the light day and the darkness night, and the evening and the morning were the first day (*Gen* 1:3-5).

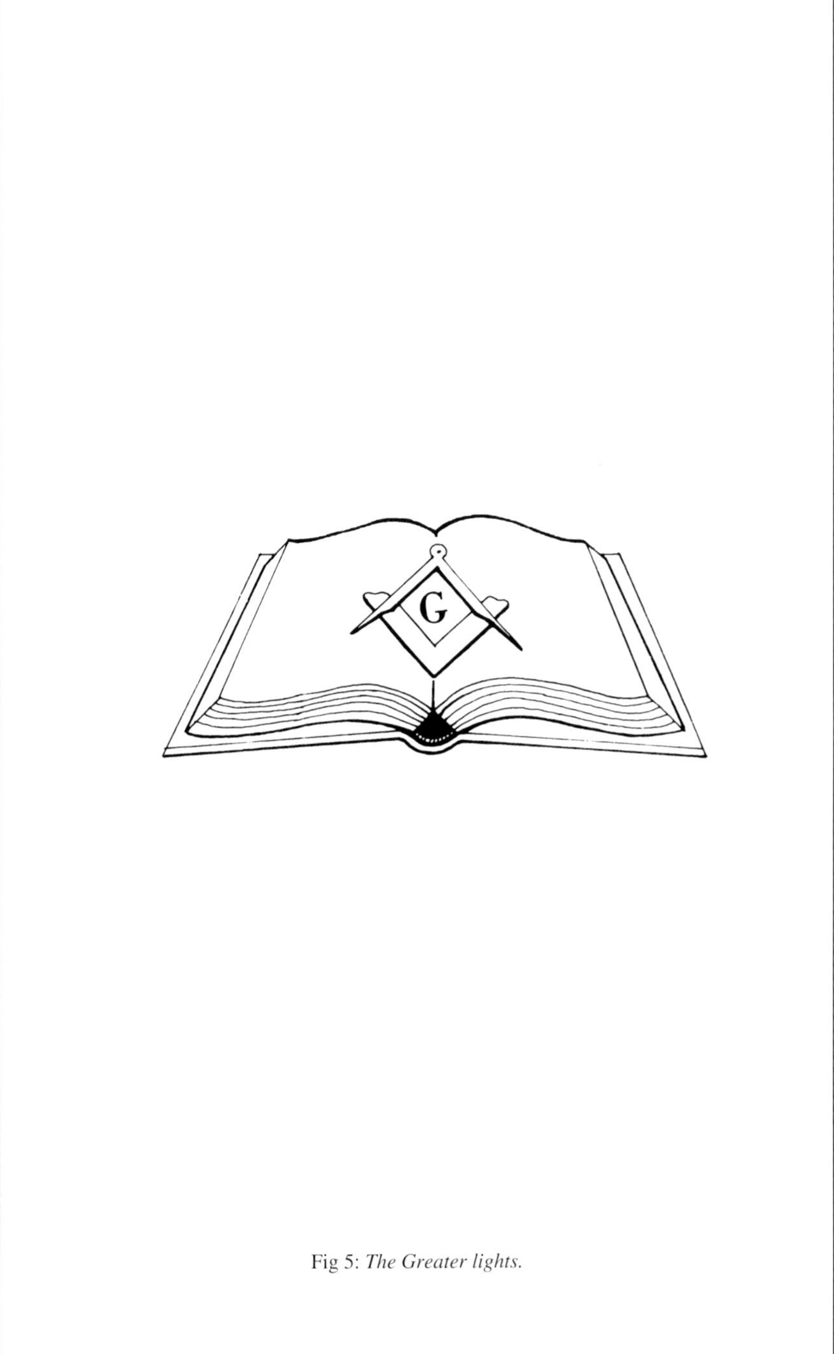

Fig 5: *The Greater lights.*

Fig 5: *The Greater lights.*

From this record in the Holy Writ, the transformation of voids into forms such as the firmament, the sea, land and all living creatures, etc took place after the creation or issuing forth of light which was the animating force. Indeed it was not until the fourth day that the sun to rule the day and give light to the earth, and the moon to govern the night and the stars were created. *What was therefore the first light created on the first day?* This has been described as the unsubstantiate primordial light, the driving force throughout creation, the primordial seed, the ever active primordial energy.

What Light Does the Mason Indeed Seek to See?

The light given in the great fiat can therefore be equated with the will of God — the creative will of God — from which all forms emanate in perfection and from which also the spirit core of man emanates in subsequent creation. This is the beginning of creation and the understanding of the place of man in creation which masonic science is out to teach. The VSL further bears testimony in retrospect in the following manner:

> In the beginning was the word, and the word was with God, and the word was God. (*St John* 1.1.)
>
> All things were made by him, and without him was not anything made that was made. (*St John* 1.3.)
>
> In him was life and the life was the light of men. And the light shineth in darkness and the darkness comprehended it not. (*St John* 1.4, 5.)

The awareness and understanding of the interconnecting cycle in creation is the knowledge that constitutes the masonic light which is darkness to the neophyte but visible to the initiated. As has been earlier mentioned, all ancient religions and esoteric sciences tend to have a relationship between physical light and mental illumination, primordial knowledge, spiritual illumination and the creative will of God. These point towards the understanding of creation which is darkness to the uninitiated.

Masonry is a science that seeks to understand creation, particularly man in relation to creation. All the tenets of moral virtue and justice in the final analysis lead to this which religion in turn calls salvation which is a belief in the immortality of the spirit.

The Mason's Quest for Understanding

The 3° in Masonry is considered to be the pinnacle of masonic manhood in Craft Masonry, including the Mark. It is also called the sublime degree because of the exalted lessons it teaches about God and a future life. At this stage, it is represented emblematically by the compasses indicating that the Mason is considered to have attained the spiritual revelation or awareness through the light. The light at this stage is described in the rituals as *DARKNESS VISIBLE* serving only to express that gloom which rests on the prospect of futurity. The gloom is further described as a mysterious veil which the eye of human reason, or the intellect, cannot penetrate unless assisted by the light which is from above. Even this is described as a glimmering ray which merely enables us to perceive our inevitable destiny and to guide our reflections to an understanding of the inner meaning of life and a knowledge of ourselves. It is the understanding and awareness of this science and our ability to lift the veil which constitutes the inner light which is darkness to the profane but visible to the worthy mason.

In this degree, we are again emblematically reminded of the significance of light by the Dormer as an ornament of the lodge. We are admonished that the Dormer typifies the Divine Radiance without which the Holy of Holies itself would be in impenetrable darkness, and bids us lift our eyes to that source of light which reveals to us the hidden mysteries, the mysterious truths which emanate from the centre of all.

In the 3° candidates are further admonished that the square pavement as an ornament symbolizes the world, and teaches us to work through life with all its varied and chequered experiences, trusting in the unbounded wisdom and goodness of THE MOST HIGH who designed and governs all. In the course of his wandering through this intricate journey, he naturally comes across certain concepts which are part of creation, and which are not readily comprehensible to him through the power of his intellect unless assisted by the light from above, which is here described as the unbounded wisdom and goodness of THE MOST HIGH. Concepts such as the world, the universe, the earth, divinity, infinity, spirit, soul, heaven, birth, death, God have not been easily comprehensible to mankind and have therefore constituted darkness to mankind to the extent that they are now understood. They are all concepts by which we are enabled the more to understand creation, and provide the answers to the masonic questions of whence came you and whither are you directing your course? Once the mason, through his daily endeavour, has crossed the threshold of understanding of these basic truths, he acquires the knowledge and wisdom which is 'Darkness Visible'. To the mason who has thus acquired this standard of illumination it is darkness visible when he looks at it subjectively but light invisible when he looks at it objectively in relation to the uninitiated.

At masonic manhood in the 3° the mason asserts that he is directing his course to the west to seek for that which was lost and which he hopes to find with the centre. He is further constantly reminded that in this journey to the west masons always meet on the level. Masonically, these expressions have a spiritual import. Since we believe in the futurity of life we believe in the immortal gift which is the Divine Spark, the emanation of the creative will, or the spirit which is the CENTRE from whence we also derive our perceptive faculties. This immortal gift is equal in every human being and never loses its lustre. It may be dimmed by the activities of the intellect through material desires, instinct, feelings, sensuality, etc but no sooner are we able to brush these stifling effects aside than the lustre springs back like a flaming fire. In this lies the principles of meeting on the level and finding the lost word with the centre, the point of equality is the immortal spark in man from whence the mason cannot err. Meeting on the level is therefore the spiritual interpretation of the equality of the divine spark in man. How we progress is then dependent on merit and ability which is the use we are able to make of our perceptive faculties, those talents wherewith God has blessed us to His glory and the welfare of our fellow creatures.

If man fails it is always his own fault, and never because of the strength or weakness of his particular gifts, for the fundamental gift, the actual power, the strongest part of man, which is the bearer and centre of all life and immortal is given to all alike. This fundamental gift is never dimmed or tarnished. It remains pure even among the greatest debasement and filth. Man only need remove the veil he has created, or discover the centre, and it will flare up again pure and unsullied as it was in the beginning as we received it.

It may also be asked why the mason had to travel from east to west to seek for that which was lost by the untimely death of our Master and what is the symbolic import of his death in the allegory which has now constituted the bedrock of craft Masonry.

It is believed that mankind shut itself off from the centre by no longer heeding its perceptive intuition which is spiritual and therefore near to God. This having arisen from the over development of and reliance on his intellect is the fall of man which is also the origin of hereditary sin. It is this same doctrine that the allegory of Adam and Eve also tries to illustrate. It is also called the Inner Voice which gives us a first impression at meeting people for the first time thus building in us sentiments of affinity, repugnance, indifference, etc. This is so because our intuitive perception, not being limited to time and space, is homogeneous with the spiritual and recognizes the true nature of the other party at a time too early for the intellect to be called into play.

By discovering the centre which is 'darkness visible' we not only overcome the fall of man but are once again in unity with our intuitive perception which is not limited to time and space, and being spiritual permits us to understand the beyond.

From the foregoing it is evident that true knowledge is light; wisdom is light, ignorance is darkness. All those who unfortunately merely submit to the intellect wanting only those things to be considered justified and correct which can be absolutely substantiated through the intellect are narrow-minded and bound inseparably to gross matter. For where does man's knowledge end? It is expanding daily even in the gross material world. Even though creation is complete and perfect, we are permitted to acquire the knowledge for its full appreciation day by day and therefore to ask for substantiation of knowledge as a structure is not true knowledge but dry or lifeless knowledge. Science, regrettably, sometimes has fallen into this predicament of producing dry scholarship. All changes that appear to take place in the material world are parts of the eternal motion causing disintegration and reforming, as nothing new can be added to creation. Man's knowledge even of his surroundings expands daily, sometimes even by ordinary discoveries. When this happens the new knowledge becomes light, while the portion yet unknown is darkness. This limitation relates only to the discoverer, for to the rest of the world even that which is light to the discoverer, clearly visible to him, is darkness.

Therefore at all material times the light which the mason is permitted to perceive that is anchored on the unity of God and the immortality of the soul, is *DARKNESS VISIBLE.*

6

LANDMARKS OF THE ORDER

To maintain and uphold the landmarks is the peculiar province of the Master, for his is the responsibility of handing over his Lodge pure and unsullied.

ONCE IN EVERY year, every properly constituted lodge elects an expert brother to preside over it, his customary duties being to rule and govern the lodge. Before he ascends the throne of King Solomon, the Master elect assents to certain ancient charges among which is the following: 'It is not in the power of any man or body of men to make alterations or innovations in Freemasonry'. He also declares his obligation among others as follows: 'That while in the chair, I will not permit nor authorize any deviation from the ancient customs and landmarks of the Craft, recognized by the Grand Lodge'.

These assurances relate to the preservation of what are known masonically as the landmarks of the order, the peculiar province of the Master, enabling him to fulfil his responsibility to hand over his lodge pure and unsullied to his successor at the end of his term of office.

In ancient times it was customary to mark the boundaries of land with stone pillars, the removal of which by unauthorized persons constituted a heinous crime to which serious sanctions attached. Accordingly, the Jewish law states, 'Thou shalt not remove thy neighbours' landmarks which they of old time have set in thine inheritance'.

In similar manner, in certain traditional African cultures where land in its physical form is regarded as the most valuable possession, second only to children, its boundaries have always been carefully protected with landmarks not in stone but evergreens of different species. In modern times even with improved techniques in cartography, the production of plans has still not done away with the practice of establishing physical landmarks in the form of beacons, etc, for the purpose of delineating boundaries. These have come to be regarded as the distinguishing characteristic of land ownership, the unauthorized alteration of which now attracts serious legal sanctions. It is obvious that the efforts and seriousness attached to the establishment of these landmarks is an index of the importance that man attaches to the ownership of land in his socio-economic environment. It is also an index of his desire to protect land from intrusion, called trespass in legal parlance.

Masonry, an esoteric science veiled in allegory and illustrated by symbols, has several distinguishing appendages attached to it. These may be in the form of ceremonies and rites, jewels and furniture, usages and customs, ornaments and regalia, Grand Lodge laws and by-laws, rites and regulations, etc. Even though these tend to distinguish and separate masons from the profane world, they are not all of universal application in Masonry and cannot therefore all qualify to be denominated as landmarks. It is the universal language and laws by which masons are separated from the profane world which constitute the landmarks of the order and not local ceremonies, laws and usages, no matter how masonic they may appear. To attempt to remove or alter these sacred landmarks by which masons universally examine and prove a brother's claim to participation in the privileges is one of the most serious offences that a mason can commit.

It is accepted that the classification of what should be regarded as landmark and what should not has caused great controversy among masonic writers. The best yardstick in my view should be those usages and customs, symbols, laws, etc that can stand the test of universal application, not only by virtue of their long usage, whether in oral custom or codified practice, but by virtue of their being so fundamental to the philosophy of Freemasonry that without them the order will cease to be Freemasonry.

The main characteristics and peculiar prerequisites of a landmark in Freemasonry would appear to be threefold:

(a) The usage or practice must be of universal application in Freemasonry wherever it is practised, and must be distinguishable as relating to nothing but Freemasonry.

(b) The usage or practice where it is not codified must relate to antiquity as being traceable to the time when the memory of man runneth not to the contrary.

(c) The usage or practice must be unrepealable, as it is not in the power of any man or body of men to make alterations or innovations in Freemasonry. It must have the character of the law of the Medes and Persians.

Even with these characteristics, there would appear to be no general agreement. There is no disagreement between authorities on the fundamental masonic law, and the ancient usages and customs are equally universally accepted. But there is no universally accepted list of landmarks. Albert G. Mackay in his masonic jurisprudence considers a list of 25 while Roscoe Pound in his masonic jurisprudence considers a list of seven. Brother Joseph Fort Newton considers a list of only five, while some of the 49 Grand Lodges in the United States of America have up to 50 or 60. Indeed, the Masonic Service Association of the United States in May 1932 issued a Digest of ancient landmarks of the Grand Lodges of the United States which was revised, brought up to date and reissued in January 1940. It contains what the different Grand Lodges have decided on the question of what is and what is not a landmark.

Antiquity alone does not also appear to constitute a landmark. The old manuscript — the Regis, Harleian, Antiquity, the oldest documents in Freemasonry, contain laws, regulations, etc which are very ancient and yet do not constitute landmarks, while the three degree structure which is comparatively new, dating from 1717, is accepted as a landmark.

Several masonic writers and thinkers have offered definitions of landmarks:

Albert G. Mackay:	*Masonic Jurisprudence*
Chetwode Crawley:	*ArsQC Vol XXIII*
Luke A. Lockwood:	*Masonic Law and Practice*
Robert Morris:	*Dictionary of Freemasonry*
Josiah Drummond:	*Maine Masonic Text Book*
Revd George Oliver:	*Dictionary of Symbolic Masonry*
John W. Simons:	*Principles of Masonic Jurisprudence*

In spite of any controversies that are discernable from the definitions as to what constitutes a landmark it is very striking to note that all agree on what is fundamental to Freemasonry. This is clearly illustrated by Brother Shepperd in his catalogue of the views of several writers, authorities and Grand Lodges in his book *Landmarks of Freemasonry*.

The fixed characteristics of landmarks preserve their sanctity, but this would appear to be in conflict with the philosophy of Masonry being a progressive science, for what is progressive cannot be static. It would appear also that it is because the science is accepted as progressive that we are admonished to extend our researches into the more hidden mysteries. If we have to reconcile this conflict, the list of what can qualify as landmarks in Freemasonry seems to be very small, and may not go much beyond Faith, Hope and Charity.

The first attempt at any comprehensive enumeration of the landmarks in Freemasonry was by Mackay in 1858 in his article 'The Foundations of Masonic Law' published in the American quarterly review of Freemasonry (Vol II, p230). These were subsequently incorporated in his text book on masonic jurisprudence, whence we deduce that there are 25 main classifications of the landmarks in Freemasonry which may be stated as follows, even though not all are of general application outside American practice.

1. Tyling

Every Lodge when duly constituted must be properly tiled to keep off Cowans and eavesdroppers from participation in our secrets. Being esoteric, the science has always had this protective need from ancient times and therefore constitutes a landmark which is never ignored.

2. The Modes of Recognition

From ancient times Freemasonry the world over has always had modes of recognition which are of universal application and which have constituted themselves into the most legitimate landmark in Freemasonry.

3. The Governance of the Master and His Two Wardens

From ancient times whenever a Lodge is properly constituted, its governance is the sole responsibility of the Master who rules supreme and his two Wardens. This constitutes a landmark of the Craft. No congregation of Masons under any other structure of governance such as a president and vice president, a chairman and vice chairman, etc would be recognised as a masonic lodge. The presence of these officers is as important to the validity of the assembly as the 'Charter of Constitution' or 'The Warrant'. Even where the names of these officers are not exactly identical by virtue of the difference in language, their number, duties, prerogative and responsibilities are identical.

4. The Basic Three Degree Structure

The basic structure of Craft Masonry is made up of three degrees, the Entered Apprentice, the Fellow Craft and Master Mason and this has become a landmark of the craft that is better preserved than most others.

This structure was further set by the solemn enactment of the United Grand Lodge of England in 1813 that ancient craft Masonry is made up of only the degrees of Entered Apprentice, Fellow of Craft and Master Mason including the Royal Arch. Even though the quest for innovation had for some time created a want of uniformity and universal application in other degrees, including those practised in France and Germany, the landmark of the three craft degrees has been maintained faithfully.

5. *The Lodge as a Unit and Place For Labour*

It has been customary from time immemorial both in operative and speculative Masonry for masons to congregate from time to time at an appointed place for labour. These congregations which are known as lodges have become a landmark of the craft.

The custom, particularly in operative Masonry where meetings were called for special purposes, dissolved and brethren departed to meet again at other times and other places, has now been changed particularly in speculative Masonry, with certainty of time and place constituting the landmark.

6. *The Legend of the 3°*

Masonry throughout the world is based on the legend of the building of a temple, King Solomon's Temple, whose symbolic import means the building of a spiritual temple. From this arose the legend of the untimely death of the Master Architect, Haram Abif, which is the bedrock of the third degree practised in all lodges, whatever language or variations in the lectures. The universality of this legend and its symbolic reference to the immortality of the soul constitutes one of the most important landmarks.

7. *Making Masons at Sight*

The prerogative of the Grand Master particularly in American practice to make masons at sight, technically defined as the power to initiate, pass and raise candidates in a Lodge of emergency known in the Constitution as an 'Occasional Lodge', convened by him and consisting of such Master Masons as he deems fit, is also an acknowledged landmark of the craft. The lodge ceases to exist as soon as the labour is over. Despite various views to the contrary, the exercise of this right by several Grand Masters appears in the Constitution.

In 1731 Lord Lovell as Grand Master formed an occasional Lodge at Houghton Hall, Sir Robert Walpole's house in Norfolk, and there made the Duke of Lorraine, later Emperor of Germany, and the Duke of Newcastle Master Masons. Similarly, by the special dispensation of the Earl of Darnley, Grand Master, Frederick Prince of Wales was initiated, passed and raised in 1737 by Dr Desaguliers who was a Past Grand Master, in an Occasional Lodge. It is also on record that in 1766 the Duke of Gloucester was initiated, passed and raised in an Occasional Lodge convened for that purpose by Lord Blaney who was then Grand Master.

8. The Authority of the Grand Master Over the Fraternity

It is an acknowledged custom that the government of the fraternity is under the supreme authority of the Grand Master elected from the body of the brethren. This is also a landmark of the Craft. The position of the Grand Master or any equivalent title performing the same functions existed in the records of the institution before the establishment of the Grand Lodges and thus does not owe its existence to any law or regulation of the Grand Lodge as may be erroneously supposed.

9. Dispensation for Opening and Holding Lodges

It is also an established custom accepted universally that the Grand Master may grant dispensation for opening and holding Lodges and that any sufficient number of masons granted such dispensation may also have the privilege of meeting and conferring degrees within the competence of such lodges. The prerogative of the Grand Master to grant such dispensation is a landmark of the institution, and the lodges established under such prerogative powers are known as 'lodges under dispensation'.

10. The Grand Master's Prerogative to Preside Over Meetings

Just as the governance of the fraternity under the supreme authority of the Grand Master is accepted as a landmark of the institution, so is his prerogative to preside over all meetings of the Craft wherever and whenever convened. It is his prerogative to assume the chair even at meetings of daughter lodges wherever and whenever he happens to be present, as it is equally customary for him to assume the chair at all Grand Lodge communications. This prerogative which is a landmark of the institution derives from ancient usage.

11. Dispensation for Conferring Degrees at Irregular Times

It is the prerogative of the Grand Master to grant dispensations for the conferring of degrees at irregular times, no matter what probation periods are prescribed by the statutes. The Grand Master would appear to have possessed this right even before the statutes were codified and since no statute can limit this prerogative, it becomes a very important landmark of the institution.

It is for this reason that a candidate can be initiated, passed and raised the same day in exercise of the prerogative of the Grand Master.

12. The Derivation of a Speculative Science from an Operative Art

It is universally accepted that Masonry as a speculative science has its basic foundation in the operative art of masons at least if not morally, largely symbolic. It is based on the legend of the building of King Solomon's Temple which is morally symbolic of the building of a spiritual temple. In the teaching of the moral truths of the Order the symbolic base is found in the artists, the materials, the implements and the plans employed in the operative building of the legendary temple. These have ben so ingrained in the body of the Order that to attempt to remove any of them would result in the destruction of the whole basis of the Order. This concept of the growth of the speculative nature of our science from the operative art of building constitutes one of the important landmarks of our Order.

13. The Right of Representation at Grand Lodge Communications

It is the inherent right of every Mason to be represented at all general meetings of the Craft, and to instruct his representatives. These general meetings held once a year are now called 'Grand Lodge Communications' and because the Craft has now grown extensively in area and number it is not practicable to exercise this prerogative individually. For this reason only the Masters and Wardens of the daughter lodges are summoned to represent brethren of their lodges. This inherent right of representation is a landmark of the craft. In the case of Scottish Masonry, it has always been limited to the Master and Wardens; or their deputies and certain other ex-officio members.

14. The Secrecy or Secret Nature of the Institution

The foundation of the organisation and practice of the institution is based on secrecy. This has been practised from the very beginning of the institution and constitutes one of the most important landmarks. There has been controversy based on social pressure over whether the society itself is secret, or whether it is a society with secrets that require protection. No matter what the correct interpretation, it is incontrovertible that the strength of the institution lies to a large extent in its secrecy. Any attempt to leave the institution of the philosophy of its tenets open will lead to a destruction of the basic character of the Order and to its death, as it would cease to be Freemasonry.

15. The Right of Every Freemason to Appeal

One of the most important attributes of the Order is the practice of every moral and social virtue, thus enabling truth and justice to guide all actions of brethren. These qualities are collectively protected in the Order by the right of every mason to appeal against the decision of his brethren in Open Lodge to the Grand Lodge on all matters affecting him, particularly on matters dealing with his expulsion, etc. This has become a highly essential landmark securing the preservation of justice and the prevention of oppression in the administration of the Craft.

16. All Masons Meet on the Level

It is acknowledged in Masonry that distinctions among men are necessary for the preservation of discipline and subordination. It is also part of the practice that monarchs, traditional rulers, obas, ananyanabos, noblemen and men of other distinctions are given respect commensurate with their different stations in life. However, when masons do meet, they meet on the level, on the understanding that all are equal and travelling on a common spiritual path which recognizes inner enlightenment, merit and ability, virtue and inner knowledge as the distinguishing characteristics and not wealth or social status. When the labours of the evening are over and brethren resume interchange with the outside world, then each will resume his social status and privileges.

17. The Right of Masonic Visitation

All properly constituted lodges wherever they may be are considered part of one universal masonic family. Consequently, every brother in good standing has the right to visit and sit in every *regular* Lodge and participate in the ceremonies. This prerogative which is known as 'the right of visitation' is a vital landmark of the Order. In accordance with custom, no mason in good standing could be refused admission when he knocks at the door of a regular Lodge, unless he has forfeited such right by virtue of his behaviour or other recognized reasons. (See paragraph 19.)

18. The VSL as One of The Great Though Emblematical Lights as an Indispensable Furniture

Masonry does not attempt to interfere with any religious faith, as the only attribute is a genuine belief in the existence of a Supreme Being. As a corollary to this, therefore, Masonry believes that all religious faiths stem from the desire for a greater understanding of the will of the GAOTU.

It is also accepted that through history certain religions have accepted certain volumes as containing the revelation of the Will of the GAOTU and thus setting a standard for justice and truth, and regulating our actions by the Divine precepts contained therein. Masons over the years have accepted such volumes during labour as their spiritual tracing board and have accepted their presence in the lodge during speculative labour as indispensable. This has become a vital landmark of the Order. Accordingly, it is now denominated by masons as 'the Volume of the Sacred Law'. In Christian countries it relates to the Old and New Testaments, in Muslim countries the Koran, and in countries where Judaism is practised the Old Testament alone.

19. The Necessity to Test Visitors Unknown to The Brethren

The science being esoteric there has always been a need to protect it from profanation and to ensure participation only of qualified persons. Even though every mason has the prerogative of visitation, there has always been a need to test visitors unknown to any of the brethren or any one of them as a mason in good standing. The necessity and right to test visitors is therefore a landmark of the Order.

20. The Belief in The Resurrection to Future Life

This belief which is an important landmark of the Order runs through the philosophy of Freemasonry and is amply illustrated in the legend of the 3°, which is the stage at which the mason is considered to have attained the age of maturity and full revelation of his spiritual nature.

21. That No Lodge May interfere With The Business of Any Other Duly Constituted Lodge

It is customary that every lodge regards all other duly constituted lodges with courtesy and exhibits the spirit of fraternity towards it. Additionally the rule of the Master and his Wardens over a lodge during their tenure of office is considered supreme. It is therefore not in the interests of the fraternity for one lodge to interfere in the business of another. This is a landmark of the Order which seeks at all times to maintain the spirit of the fraternity. The doctrine of non-interference includes refraining from conferring any degree on a member of another lodge except with the express permission of the Master backed by an appropriate dispensation.

22. A Belief in The Existence of a Supreme Being

A belief in the existence of a Supreme Being usually denominated masonically as the Great Architect of the Universe, is one of the most important landmarks in Freemasonry. While the Craft does not concern itself with religious differences, it acknowledges that no man can be made a Freemason unless he believes in the existence of God and puts his trust in Him in all cases of difficulty and danger. Masonry is all about understanding the inner truths of His creation.

23. Amenability to Laws and Regulations of a Masonic Jurisdiction

It is a landmark of the Order that every Mason is amenable to the laws and regulations of the masonic jurisdiction in which he resides, and this applies even though he may not be a member of any lodge by affiliation as this does not exempt him from masonic jurisdiction.

24. Accepted Qualification of Candidates for Initiation

The qualities which make a candidate acceptable for initiation into the Order derive from a landmark of the institution. Beside his belief in a supreme being he must be a free man, of mature age and sound judgement. That means he must be a man of stable mental ability.

25. It is Not in The Power of Any Man or Body of Men

The ultimate of the landmarks is that it is not in the power of any man or body of men to make alterations or innovations in Freemasonry. That means that the landmarks are unalterable, like the law of the

Medes and Persians, until time is no more. We are bound by the most solemn obligation to transmit them pure and unsullied to our successors as we received them from our predecessors.

These landmarks have stood the test of time even when Masonry has been seriously tested by social pressures. Time may pass but the landmarks remain long as Masonry remains. Since Masonry deals with the science of the immortality of the soul its philosophy will remain immortal even though the symbols may disappear.

Finally, in my view, to qualify as a landmark in Freemasonry, the usage or custom must have the joint characteristics of fundamentality, universality, unrepealability and antiquity. Accordingly, what constitutes the baseline of landmarks in Freemasonry can be reduced to three: faith, hope and charity. Faith in the will and unity of God, anchored on the sacred writings in the VSL; hope in the futurity of life anchored on the Hiramic Legend, and charity expressed in brotherly love. If we dare remove any of these qualities, then what is left is no more Freemasonry, and indeed it is not in the power of many or body of men to alter or derogate from any of these characteristics that form the fundamental fabric of Freemasonry.

Roscoe Pound in his own words defined landmarks in the following manner: 'Certain universal, unalterable and non-repealable fundamentals which have existed from time immemorial, and are so thoroughly a part of Freemasonry that no masonic authority may derogate from them or do aught but maintain them'.

7

UNSHAKEN FIDELITY IN THE 'SACRED TRUSTS'

We are bound by duty and ancient custom at the end of labour and the beginning of regular contact to lock up the secrets of the Order in a safe repository uniting in the the act of fidelity that neither permits evasion nor equivocation.

Introduction

THROUGHOUT HISTORY THINGS of value have been preserved with some element of secrecy and the keeping of them has always been a sacred trust reposed in appointed or even self-appointed keepers. Such things may be valued physical objects or doctrines and concepts. This secrecy appeared with the formation of the earliest human groups and communities when the frailties of human nature and the inequalities of material circumstances influenced people's conduct. These sacred trusts were expected to be maintained with great fidelity.

In Masonry such fidelity is described as being without evasion, equivocation or any mental reservation whatsoever, and strengthened by obligations backed by symbolic sanctions emblematic of the wrath of the Deity in the presence of whom such obligations are taken. This is clearly illustrated to the candidate at his first admission when it is the duty of Bro Inner Guard to admonish in the following manner: 'And as this is a momentary torture to your flesh so may the recollection of it prove an everlasting torture to your *conscience* should you ever attempt to reveal the secrets of Freemasonry unlawfully'. This presupposes that in Masonry the penalties for breach of obligations of fidelity taken in the presence of the MOST HIGH are matters for the 'conscience' which, by all standards, are more excruciating than any physical or emblematic sanctions that have been symbolically stated, particularly as Masonry is a sacramental science.

Fidelity and Sacred Trusts Outside Masonry

It is probable that one of the earliest examples of the importance of fidelity in sacred trusts is symbolized in the communication of the sacred commandments to the Israelites by Moses on his descent from Mount Sinai. The Commandments, together with their explanations, were communicated first to Aaron alone, next to Aaron and his two sons Eleazar and Ithamar, next to Aaron, his two sons and the 70 elders who comprised the Sanhedrin and finally to all qualified among the common people by desire. At the commitment of the laws thereafter into writing for all to read, the explanations were left out. These were kept as a sacred trust by those who were privileged to receive them orally for further communication. Similarly, the ancient Egyptians communicated their secrets concealed in heiroglyphics to the Priests and Magii alone who were bound by oath never to reveal them. Pythagoras established his system similarly and many Orders in recent times have copied their example.

Masonry makes the right hand the symbol of fidelity borrowing from the ideals of ancient poets. Indeed, the virtue of fidelity was often symbolized by the heart in open hand on ancient medals, or more often by two hands clasped. In African mystery orders examples are found in the sacredness of similar trusts meticulously administered by the keepers of the conscience of the *Ogun Deity*, the *Ekine seki apu* Order, the *Ekpe* Order and the ceremonies of the installation of the keepers of the *Odema* which is the god of the land whose keeper is the *Obenema* or *Amanyanabo*, *Obi* or *Oba*.

In all monarchic systems, including those existing now, vows of fidelity are required of the monarch at his installation as keeper of the conscience of the land. The same is true in more modern political systems where presidents, prime ministers and ministers of state take oaths of fidelity at swearing-in ceremonies before taking up their duties. Religious orders are no exception to the rule as all bishops, cardinals and similar officials swear oaths of fidelity before assumption of office, as was done by the ancient priests.

The sacred trusts reposed in these keepers call for certain duties which they solemnly undertake to perform. These duties are instructions and guidelines for the journey through our chequered human existence, and Masonry being a living science, we are enjoined to know and understand these duties for daily application and to preserve our ancient usages and established customs sacred and inviolable, inducing others by our own example to hold them in veneration.

Masonry and The Sacred Trusts

Having now understood the background of sacred trusts and the required attendant fidelity, what are the sacred trusts in Freemasonry that masons are enjoined to preserve and to induce others by their own example to hold in veneration?

The sacred trusts reposed in freemasons would appear to be in three broad categories, conveniently described as:

(a) Trusts related to the ceremonial drama of the Order.

(b) Trusts related to rules of conduct and moral justice.

(c) Trusts related to the inner mysteries of the science and therefore esoteric and spiritual.

Ceremonial Drama

Since neither the obligations nor the admonitions and exhortations contain any specific exclusions, it is assumed that the fidelity required of us covers this category with a fair level of discretion without detriment. Under this category may be included the following:

(a) The setting of a normal lodge room, otherwise known as the temple, with its furniture, jewels and ornaments and their relative positions are to be preserved and held in veneration.

(b). The number of functions of the various office bearers in a lodge duly constituted, and their relative stations are to be preserved and maintained as a sacred trust.

(c) The mode of dress and the ceremonial drama of opening and closing the lodge are to be preserved as a sacred trust among freemasons.

(d) The orders and ceremonial content of Initiation and preferment of the degree of Fellow Craft and Master Mason are also to be preserved as a sacred trust.

(e) The duty to regard the sign, grip or token and the word in each degree as a guard to the privileges and the corresponding duty never to give the word in full except in open lLodge, demands an unshaken fidelity as masons are specifically admonished to be cautious.

(f) The badge of innocence and bond of friendship being more honourable than the Order of the Thistle or any other Order, masons are exhorted to acknowledge and never to disgrace it. They are further exhorted never to put on the badge should they be about to enter a lodge where there is a brother with whom they are at variance. They are duty bound not to disturb the harmony of the lodge.

Rules of Conduct and Moral Justice

While in general these rules also deal with the Order, they are more related to masonic conduct and moral justice. So masons by their own conduct induce others to hold them in veneration. In this category may be included the following norms generally accepted and maintained:

(a) The great and valuable privileges in Masonry are the secrets and mysteries of the Order for which vows of fidelity are required to keep inviolate and to compel masons to abide by the ancient usages and established customs of the Order. These secrets and mysteries of the Order are never to be revealed, even to a lawful brother or brethren, except after due trial, strict examination or a full conviction that he or they are worthy of that confidence.

(b) The secrets and mysteries of our Order we are not to write, carve, engrave or otherwise delineate upon anything movable or immovable, under the canopy of heaven, whereby or whereon any letter, character, or figure, or the least trace of a letter, character, or figure small become legible or intelligible to any one in the world, so that the secrets are made known unlawfully.

(c) We must support and maintain the constitution and laws of the Grand Lodge and give strict obedience to the byelaws of our Mother Lodge.

(d) The distinguishing characteristic of a Freemason's heart is charity, and the practice of charity which has the approbation of heaven and earth is a sacred trust reposed in us. In the Holy Writ we are admonished that 'It is more blessed to give than to receive', while the rituals exhort us that the practice of charity blesses him who gives as well as him who receives. To this we must add the other masonic ornament which is benevolence.

(e) The VSL we are to regard as a standard of truth and justice, as therein we are taught the duties we owe to God, to ourselves and to our neighbours.

(f) We must be exemplary in the discharge of our civic duties as citizens of the world, by avoiding subversion, by paying due obedience to the laws of any state that affords us protection and becomes the place of our residence and by giving allegiance to the sovereign of our native land.

(g) We are to act on the square with all mankind and more particularly our brother freemasons and show dedication to pursuits in life that would make us respectable, while making daily advancement in masonic knowledge.

(h) We are to supply the wants and relieve the necessities of worthy brethren to the utmost of our power, and on no account wrong them or see them wronged, but view their interests as inseparable from our own.

(i) We are to be particularly attentive to our behaviour during assemblies, as the Temple is Holy and sacred, and as the solemnity of the ceremonies requires serious deportment. It is recognized that at deeply solemn moments man tends to perceive the nearness of his God to him through the bridge thus created from the purity of his perceptive faculty to give him Divine awareness. This also happens at moments of extreme joy or deepest sorrow when briefly the purity of man's perceptive faculty is raised to its height, thus pushing aside everything earthly and low and merging with the homogeneous purity of the eternal primordial spirit or paradise which poets and prophets have been permitted under similar circumstances to perceive from time to time.

(j) We are to preserve our ancient usages and established customs sacred and inviolable and induce others by our example to hold them in veneration.

(k) We are not to palliate nor aggravate the offences of other brethren, but in the decision of every trespass against our rules we are to judge with candour, admonish with friendship and reprehend with mercy.

(l) We are to obey all lawful signs and summonses sent to us from a Master Mason's Lodge if within the length of our cable tow, and to plead no excuse save that of illness or the pressing emergency of our own public or private avocations.

(m) We are to maintain and uphold the mason's five points of fellowship in act as well as words, exemplified by true and genuine brotherhood, mutual defence and support, succour of a brother's weakness and relief of his necessities, maintenance of the secrets of a brother in the safe repository of our breasts when entrusted into our care, maintenance and preservation of a Master Mason's honour as our own, upholding a brother's good name.

(n) We are to repel the slanderer of a brother's good name, and most strictly respect the chastity of those nearest and dearest to him in the persons of his wife, his sister and his child.

(o) We are strictly to avoid the stain of falsehood and dishonour which is masonically regarded as a terror greater than that of death.

(p) We must be careful at all times to perform our allotted task while it is day, and continue to listen to the voice of nature which bears witness to the futurity of life.

(q) We are to ensure that the qualities of uprightness of conduct, humanity of disposition and energy of purpose are not applied for selfish or ambitious ends, as this would deaden the spiritual principle in us.

The Spiritual and Inner Mysteries of our Science

It is important to realise that all sacred trusts, ceremonial or rules of conduct are intended ultimately to lead to an inner understanding of the science which is spiritual. Therefore, all the other trusts are supplementary to the trusts in this category which are:

(a) As by our daily progress in Masonry we are permitted to extend our researches into the more hidden mysteries of the Craft, we are enjoined to make the hidden mysteries and nature of our science our future study, to estimate aright the wonderful manifestations of the Almighty Architect's plan.

(b) That the inner spiritual knowledge which we all strive to attain, and which would establish happiness in the paths of our lives, must be grounded in accuracy, aided by labour and prompted by education and perseverance.

(c) That the mason's attainment of a higher realisation of the immortal principle of primordial goodness must be based on square conduct, level steps and uprightness of intentions, as intentions and deeds are spiritually the same and interchangeable.

(d) That our belief in the immortality of life and our consequent faith in our ascent to the Grand Lodge above where THE MOST HIGH lives and reigns for ever must be based on acting according to the immutable spiritual laws of the DIVINE CREATOR, the VSL being at all times the guide of our faith.

The sacred trusts reposed in us all for certain great duties which we have solemnly engaged ourselves to perform. Duty, honour and gratitude bind us to these trusts, and oblige us to enforce by example and precept the tenets of our system contained in these trusts. Let no motive therefore make us swerve from our duty, violate our vows or betray our trust. Let us continue to remember the faithfulness and steadfastness of the celebrated artist who forms the core of the allegory in our belief in immortality as contained in the equally celebrated expression: 'As for himself, he would rather suffer death than betray the sacred trust reposed in him'.

As we look back on the sacred trusts outlined above, we should judge by our fidelity whether we are performing our duties as masons to the elevation of mankind, the honour of Masonry and the glory of the THE GREAT ARCHITECT OF THE UNIVERSE by whose creative fiat all things were made.

8

BROTHERHOOD: ESOTERIC AND SACRAMENTAL

The components of its outward visible part, the intermediate intellectual part and its inner spiritual part complete the circle of the esoteric nature of our science.

THROUGHOUT HISTORY MASONRY in its speculative form has been difficult to understand and therefore subject to various interpretations by individuals who are not privileged to be members, religious organisations and even governments. Its true nature and philosophy are not fully comprehended even by some members of the brotherhood, who may be vast in its organisational and structural rules and rituals as these are merely incidental to the true nature of Masonry. This is so because the brotherhood in its speculative form is esoteric and sacramental as distinct from operative Masonry practised by lodges in the guild system from which speculative Masonry is supposed to have originated in form but not in character.

The difficulty in understanding its real nature is exemplified by the different attempts made over the years to give the brotherhood a precise definition. There is however, a reassuring common strain that runs through all the definitions, and this points to the inner spiritual content that is perceived only by those who by their own endeavours have been privileged to understand.

Some of the definitions that have been given to Masonry or that can be deduced from refecting on its philosophy are as follows:

(a) Masonry is a peculiar system of morality veiled in allegory and illustrated by symbols. This is probably the best known and most popular of the definitions, propounded by Dr Hemming some 180 years ago.

(b) Masonry is a system of moral philosophy expressed in ceremonial drama — moral philosophy, being the base of the drama, makes the system spiritual and therefore not a conceived plot that is easy to unfold to its audience as theatrical drama would be.

(c) Masonry is a moral science that strives to provide the answers to the perpetual questions, 'Who am I?', 'Whence Came I?' and 'Whither Go I?'. Since the answers to all these refer to a state of being, the masonic purpose which is 'to seek for that which was lost' can only refer to spiritual revelation and awareness which is a state of being. This must also lead us to perceive that even JABULON is symbolic and allegorical.

(d) Masonry is a science that is perpetually engaged in the search after Divine Truth and which employs symbolism as its method of instruction (Mackay).

(e) Masonry is a moral system that teaches the philosophy of the inner meaning of man recognized as a human being, his place and purpose in creation, all acted in ceremonial drama and illustrated by symbols, based on allegories.

The Masonic Character

Judging from the definitions given, the true masonic character can be deduced as composed of three basic elements:

(a) An outward visible part illustrative of the drama and organisation of the craft, together with the paraphernalian attachments, including conviviality at banquet or refreshment.

(b) An intermediate intellectual part illustrative of the philosophical interpretations of the allegories, drama and symbols of the Craft which constitute the beginning of the hidden mysteries of the science. This demands a fairly substantial standard of education in the candidate.

(c) An inner spiritual part illustrative of our level of awareness, unfoldment and enlightenment based on individual endeavour and contemplation and not necessarily on intellectualism or education.

As a further illustration of the structure and true character of Masonry, these three basic elements correspond to the three degrees practiced in Craft Masonry which are the Entered Apprentice of 1°, the Fellow Craft or 2° and the Master Mason or 3°. In other words, the 1° represents the outward visible part, the 2° is illustrative of the intermediate intellectual part while the 3° is indicative of the inner spiritual part — the prospect of futurity.

Fig 6: *The Ornaments.*

It may be further added that these in a spiritual sense are also representative of the different stages of the unfoldment of the mind in its journey towards illumination. The actual moment of illumination if it is ever attained is so short and brisk that the different stages of prior unfoldment are not noticeable, but it is gratifying that Masonry makes a daily attempt to prepare the minds of its professors for the reception of this Divine Truth. Regrettably, however, most masons do not develop beyond the level of the outward visible part, and this qualifies them to be labelled 'the rough ashlar masons'.

Indeed, the practice of Masonry without an understanding of its second and third elements will render the whole system a meaningless elitist ceremonial fraud useful only for its charities which in the main are geared to its members and their dependents.

The different elements in the character of Speculative Masonry may be examined and categorised as follows, even though this attempt cannot be considered fully comprehensive.

The Outward Visible Part

In the main, these are merely incidental to the organisation of the Craft, but among the most significant of them are:

(a) The Ornaments
These are generally made up of:
- (i) the masonic pavement;
- (ii) the indented tassel, or the tasselated edge; and
- (iii) The Blazing Star or the Glory in the Centre. They are masonically regarded as ornate because they are decorations with which a properly constituted lodge should be adorned.

(b) The Furniture
Even though a properly constituted lodge contains substantial amounts of furniture in the normal sense, it is only the VSL, the square and the compasses that are regarded masonically as the furniture of the Lodge.

(c) The Jewels
These fall into three categories in every properly constituted lodge, *ie* movable jewels, immovable jewels and official jewels (jewels of office).
- (i) Movable: These comprise the square, the level and the plumb rule, and are regarded as movable by virtue of their transfer from one officer to another in succession, even though their positions in east, south and west

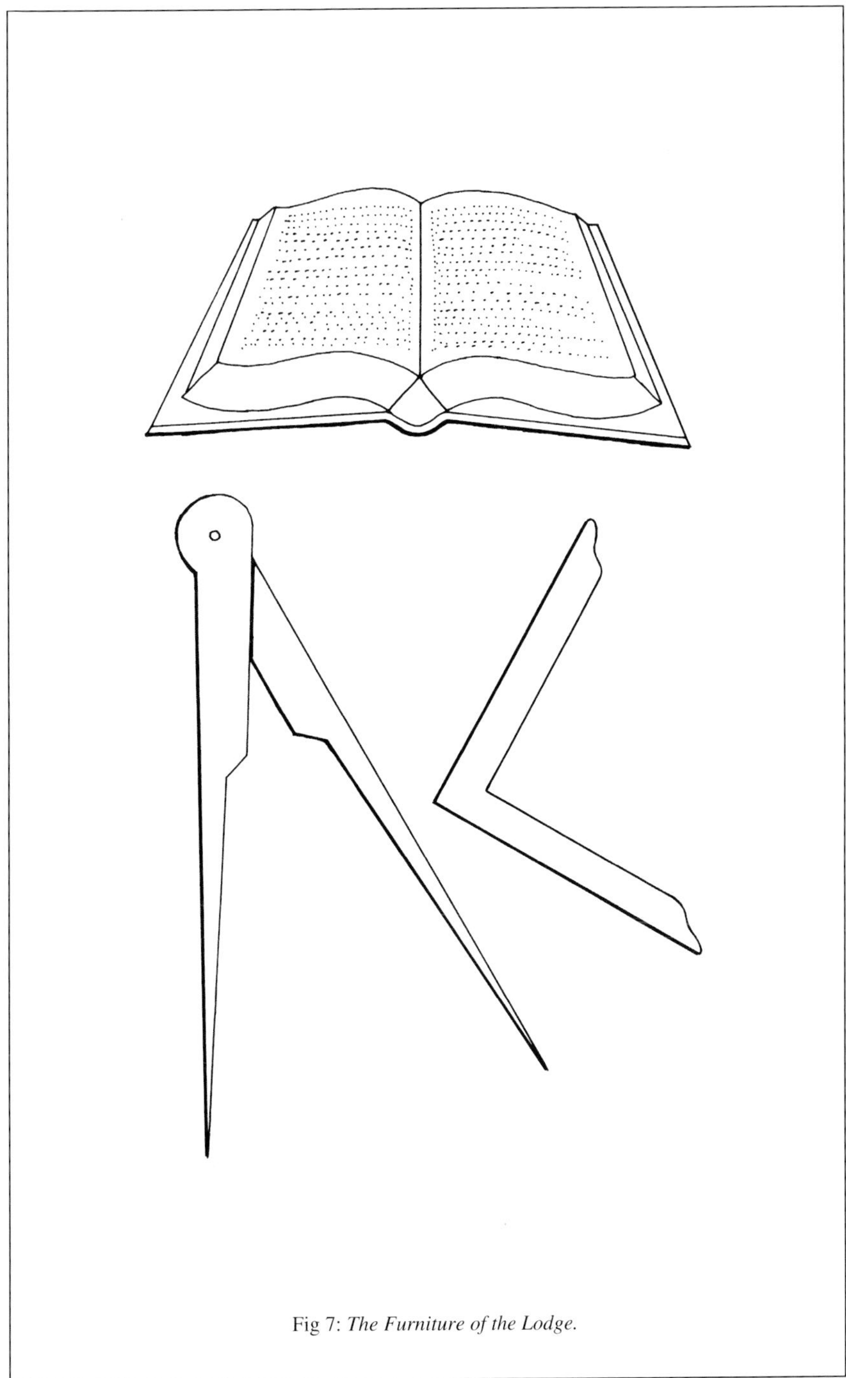

Fig 7: *The Furniture of the Lodge.*

remain constant. Indeed, because of their fixed position, the American system classifies them as immovable.

(ii) Immovable: These consist of the rough ashlar, the perfect ashlar and the tracing board. These are classified in the American system as movable jewels.

(iii) Official: These are the emblems of office worn by the different officers of the lodge as attachments to their collars of office, thus the SW wears the level, the JW the plumb, etc.

(d) The Temple

The term lodge has two connotations, the first being a body of brethren gathered for the purpose of masonic ceremonial and the second being a Lodge room which in physical terms means the temple. The temple as a building is therefore one of the most significant components of the outward visible part of speculative Masonry, particularly as the main allegory in speculative Masonry centres around the building of King Solomon's Temple. It is an acknowledged fact that wherever a masonic temple is found the world over, it stands in regal majesty illustrative of the inner dignity and purity of purpose of the institution it represents.

(e) The Ceremonies

In Craft Masonry they consist of the three degrees of Entered Apprentice, Fellow Craft and Master Mason. The order and manner of the ceremonies, the perambulations, the rituals and even the secrets imparted are visible representations of inner truths which will unfold in later stages through the personal endeavours of the candidate. The manner in which the rituals are performed may vary but they are all the outward visible part of Masonry.

(f) The Mode of Dress

The mode of dress permitted at the attendance of any lodge meeting is usually strictly formal wherever Masonry is practiced. This is not merely an elitist practice, but a physical and visible representation of the cleanliness and purity of the body. The apron, the sash, the gauntlet, the collar, the white gloves and the jewels which physically adorn the mason are visible representations of inner spiritual truths, not easily recognisable even by some masons, let alone the profane outside world.

(g) The Symbols

Among this group may be included the signs, tokens and words, and the working tools in all the degrees, which are outward

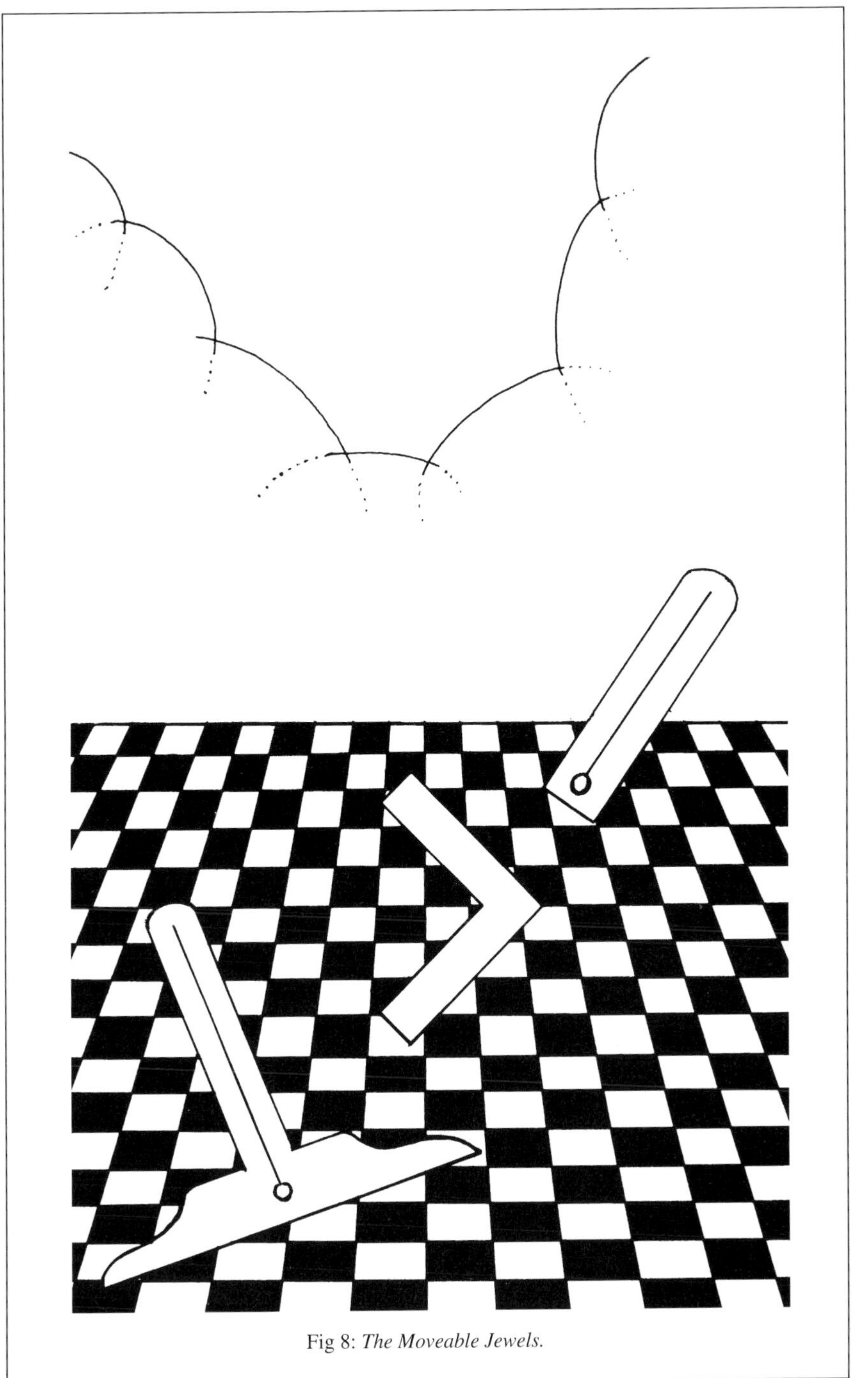

Fig 8: *The Moveable Jewels.*

visible representations of inner truths, which we are entitled to discover through our research.

(h) The Charities
These and the benevolent organisations are an outward representation of the character of the institution, but they also serve to illustrate the distinguishing characteristic of a freemason's heart. Examples of these in a collective way are the masonic hospitals and schools, etc.

(i) The Masonic Banquet
Refreshment after labour is a recognized practice in Masonry and for that reason every standard Temple has a banquet hall. The conviviality is mixed with masonic lessons, and these together with the general character of the banquet are also merely the outward visible part of Masonry.

(j) The Working Tools
The working tools in Craft Masonry in each degree are virtually the same wherever you may go, and constitute some of the most important outward visible part of Freemasonry, particularly in the ceremonials.

(k) The Masonic Manner of Speech
In a rather unconscious way Masonry gives to its professors a manner of speech that is cautious and exemplary and easily recognizable by all masons. This is probably acquired from the language of the rituals and it has constituted one of the important outward visible attributes of Freemasonry.

(l) The Meeting Times
Masonic meetings are usually held in the evening, masonically described as when the sun is at its meridian. This has also become one of the outward visible parts of Masonry.

(m) The Allegories
The esoteric character of Masonry is veiled in the allegories which are the same wherever Masonry is practiced regularly. They form the basis of the ceremonies and have therefore become one of the most important outward visible parts of Freemasonry. Some of these allegories are so vivid that some masons have not been able to distinguish them from the inner truths they are supposed to teach.

(n) The Office Bearers
The practice universally is that no lodge can be regularly constituted without the Master and his two Wardens. The other office bearers may vary in number and designation according to the

constitution but the presence of office bearers is an important outward visible part of the Craft.

(o) The Constitution and laws
Obedience to the constitution and laws of the Grand Lodge and compliance with the bye-laws of the lodge are necessary requirements which also constitute an important aspect of the outward visible part of the Craft.

The Intermediate Intellectual Part

As has been mentioned earlier, the intermediate intellectual element in the masonic character is illustrative of the philosophical interpretations of the allegories, drama, symbols and the whole structure that constitutes the hidden mysteries of the science. It is the beginning of the path towards understanding the spiritual nature of the Craft, and this path as far as Masonry is concerned demands a fair level of intellectual appreciation. This does not mean that there can be no spiritual revelation and awareness without intellectual capacity but the unfolding of the veil of symbolism does require intellectual and philosophical appreciation where speculative Masonry is concerned.

I believe it is for this reason that the beauty and depth of esoterism in the rituals and practice of the Craft cannot be unravelled by some masons even after having completed the three Craft degrees, or even after having the privilege of passing through King Solomon's Throne in these days.

The structure of the ceremonials, particularly in the 2°, bears testimony to this assertion and shows that this degree is the beginning of the philosophical understanding of Masonry, as can be illustrated by the following passages:

(a) At the opening of the lodge in this degree, the JW asserts that he should be proved by the square, an angle of 90° or the fourth part of a circle. This assertion leaves unanswered questions: Why is it a square or the fourth part of a circle? What are the other three parts of the circle?

(b) The prayer at the opening supplicates the GAOTU 'that the rays of Heaven may shed their benign influence to enlighten us in *the path of virtue and science*'. Clearly the enlightenment requested is *in the path* which is the beginning of the knowledge of the science of the Craft.

(c) The password in this degree, which is 'S', symbolises 'plenty' and is depicted by an ear of corn near a fall of water. Philosophically this signifies that at the beginning of the ascent to spiritual heights we must be able to conquer self as symbolised by plenty. In other words, the mason asserts that he has passed beyond recognition of material poverty and the lure of unnecessary material desires which could stifle or impede his attempts at spiritual ascent. The symbol of plenty is therefore a shield for our defence.

(d) His advance towards his spiritual rewards is by a winding staircase illustrating the intellectual effort required in the ascent which begins in this degree.

(e) In the admonition after his obligation, it is clearly stated that the disclosure of one point of the compasses merely implies that a new beam of light has been shed upon his life to enable him to *discover the way* to that knowledge which he would attain. Again this points out that this degree is the beginning of his knowledge, *the discovery of the way*.

(f) At the investiture, the candidate is further admonished that he is expected to make the hidden mysteries and the nature of the science his future study, that he may be enabled the better to discharge his duties as a freemason.

(g) His SE charge admonishes in the following manner: 'You will now be permitted to extend your researches into the more hidden mysteries of the Craft'. Again this clearly shows that it is at this stage that he is permitted to extend his researches intellectually into the more hidden mysteries. How does he do this?

(h) In the presentation of the working tools, the candidate is clearly admonished to have hope in the attainment of a higher realisation of that immortal principle from whence all goodness emanates, and that this attainment can only come by square conduct and level steps.

(i) In his charge he is finally admonished that he shall find the study of masonic science a valuable branch of education tending to polish and adorn the mind, especially its hidden or symbolic meaning which, being of a Divine and moral nature, is enriched with the most useful and inspiring knowledge.

We thus find that this is the degree in which we are equipped to ponder on the outward visible part of Freemasonry and in this process of reflection we then find that wisdom, strength and beauty are symbolically represented by the Master and his two Wardens. We also find that while the Temple represents the world in a wide sense, it also symbolically represents man as the spiritual Temple, in similar manner to the parable of the destruction of the Temple and its rebuilding in three days in the VSL.

Fig 9: *The Winding Staircase.*

We also find that the squaring of the lodge, which is a regular practice, is symbolically representative of the spiritual entry of man into his earthly existence and his departure from it, and the need for patience, regularity and uprightness in his path towards spiritual progress. We find that Jacob's ladder which is symbolically representative of our levels of spiritual unfoldment has its base as the VSL given to us as the standard of truth.

We find that the password of 'S' and 'T' in the 2° and 3° refer to 'plenty' and 'worldly possessions'. These are symbolically representative of the desire to conquer self for the purpose of spiritual ascent. It is a state in which we are detached from the love of worldly desires and not necessarily a rejection of material things. In effect this means that, while worldly possessions are not a qualification for our spiritual ascent, they must not be an impediment because once we possess them they no longer demand attention which we should devote to our spiritual elevation.

We discover also that the winding staircase and the square pavement are symbolically illustrative of the intricacies of our chequered and varied experiences through our earthly existence. The mason at this stage is at the winding staircase at the beginning of the porchway or entrance to the Temple, after he had passed through the two great pillars of strength and stability. He represents the beginning of our journey through life, confronting this great task of self-improvement for which, if he performs faithfully, a reward awaits him. The difficulties of the development of his moral and intellectual character for the attainment of Divine Truth through the rough sands of time are represented by the winding staircase, while the password and the wages are the symbols of the conquest of selfish desire to lighten our ascent.

The intermediate intellectual part is therefore the beginning of the esoteric character, that secret portion of Masonry known only to true initiates, as distinct from exoteric or monitorial Masonry which is open and accessible to all who desire to read the manuals and published works of the Order which are abundant.

The Inner Spiritual Part

It has already been stated that the inner spiritual part of Masonry is based on individual endeavour and contemplation and not necessarily on intellectualism or education. It is indicative of a personal level of enfoldment, enlightenment and awareness of the fundamental unity from which all religions spring. Masonry, being not a religion but an organization that cuts across all religions, forms a basis for the understanding of this fundamental unity. This understanding is not based on

Fig 10: *The First Degree Tracing Board.*

charity, benevolence, alms-giving or even the cultivation of social virtues which have the approbation of Heaven and earth, for these are merely incidental to the organization. Similarly, it is not based on our ability to recite the rituals and work the ceremonies for these are perfunctory incidents of the outward visible part. It is related to the genuineness of our search and desire for the Divine Truth — the Centre — and that truth is the unity of God and the immortality of the soul. In this search the various degrees are stages of initiation indicating the different stages through which the human mind passes in its unfoldment and the many difficulties which we must encounter individually or collectively in our progress from ignorance or darkness to the acquisition of this truth or light which emanates from the centre of all (*Mackay*, Vol 1, p209).

Masonry believes that nature or creation is not an accidental or fortuitous occurrence of atoms and therefore teaches man to understand and act in accordance with his established rightful place in the scheme of the Universe. That place may be a combination of what he occupies now and what he occupies next.

The various tenets and principles of Masonry are therefore designed to maintain harmony in our surroundings in what we occupy now and to assist our ascent to what we occupy next in fulfilment of the grand design of the Creator.

9

THE TEMPLE — ITS MASONIC COMPONENTS AND CONTENTS

A combination of design, orientation, components, and contents creates a hallowed atmosphere for worship capable of transporting its participants spiritually and reminds us of the rectitudes of our life and actions as the components of the moral temple that we seek to build regarding which King Solomon's Temple is merely symbolic.

THIS CHAPTER IS written so that we may ask ourselves when next we visit a masonic temple whether we are sufficiently conscious of our surroundings and whether we have hitherto been as observant as we should be. The chapter deals with the Temple, its physical components and contents, not the philosophical or spiritual meanings to which they relate unless this is absolutely necessary, as they have been discussed in other parts of this book.

Many masons, even of considerable masonic age, do not know the names, meanings or even the relative positions of some of the masonic objects forming the components and contents of the lodge they regularly attend. This appalling but widespread ignorance is attributable to many causes, the most common in my opinion being:

(a) Frustrated Expectations — Even though we are admonished to extend our researches, most masons show lack of concern. This is generally caused by frustrated expectations. Many candidates get admitted with the expectation of social and material benefits, and of the immediate acquisition of spiritual knowledge through regular instruction. As they do not readily find these, they develop a lack of concern which makes them insensitive to the responsibility of being conscious of their masonic surroundings.

(b) Mixed Sentiments of Fear and Shame — Some masons are inhibited from making enquiries about these objects from a mixture of fear and shame. They wrongly develop the feeling that other masons assume that they know or ought to know and therefore become either afraid or ashamed to make enquiries of their brethren. So long as the feeling of fear and shame lasts, so long will the mason continue to live in ignorance, as no regular opportunity arises when these lessons are taught.

(c) Vanity of Ambition — There is no doubt that Masonry as an organization is regarded with great respect, dignity and sometimes fear by the outside world. This respect and dignity stem from the calibre of its membership. Respect and dignity are also earned by the comportment and achievements of individual members in the societies in which they live. Fear, on the other hand, arises from the secrecy and mystery attached to the organization. Some masons regrettably find deep satisfaction in being associated with the Craft, simply to attach the feelings of respect, dignity and fear to their empty egos. This vanity of ambition and purpose makes them insensitive to their surroundings and they therefore make little progress as they consider mere membership a fulfilment of their ambition.

(d) Paucity of Knowledge among Fellow Brethren — Young masons often find themselves in a predicament at the beginning of their enquiries. They find to their great disappointment that most senior brethren from whom they are supposed to learn do not themselves know much, but instead of accepting their ignorance often come up with the bluff of requesting the young mason to extend his researches, as if he is not one source of the research.

(e) Absence of Regular Instruction — The pressure of modern life makes it difficult for lodges to organise regular instructions and consequently young masons are left with the opportunity of attending only regular meetings, including emergencies. These meetings, which are usually not more that four in the month, are devoted to the formal business of the Lodge, and conferment of degrees — and there is therefore no opportunity to learn more than is contained in the ceremonies. library facilities are also in general very scanty in proportion to the spread of Masonry over the four quarters of the globe and in some countries there are none at all. The traditional belief in the protection of the secrets of the Craft makes prolific publication of materials a hazardous exercise. A combination of these factors keeps the mason ignorant of his surroundings no matter how sensitive he may be.

If Masonry must continue to maintain its place as a vehicle for assisting its professors in their path for spiritual ascent and in maintaining harmony in society through the brotherhood of man, then the organization must make conscious efforts to improve the avenues for learning and instruction related not only to its principles and tenets, but also to its basic philosophy.

It is now gratifying to note that there is now a much more healthy attitude in England and Scotland to the publication of masonic literature, as the emphasis is increasingly on masonic education, via books and lectures.

The Temple

The building of King Solomon's Temple is the most significant of the masonic allegories. For this reason masonic temples are built as miniature reflections of that temple in form. The components may be considered under the following heads:

(a) *Its dimensions and ground plan:* In the Holy Writ the dimensions of King Solomon's Temple are given in the following manner: 'And the house which King Solomon built for the Lord, the length thereof was three score cubits and the breadth thereof twenty cubits; and the height thereof thirty cubits' (I *Kings* 6:2).

It was therefore in plan a long quadrangle or oblong square with its length three times its breadth. Although it has not been possible in all cases, masonic temples have tried to keep to these dimensions if not in size at least in proportions.

(b) *Its orientation:* Wherever possible masonic temples are oriented due east-west, and when not physically possible they are symbolically considered so. The reason for this is partially found in the VSL which states that the first tabernacle to be built by Moses for the worship of the Most High after the deliverance of the children of Israel from bondage was due east-west, as was King Solomon's Temple.

Two more reasons are a reflection of the path of the sun, the Glory of God that is due east-west, and the established fact that learning started from the east and spread to the west. Learning in this case includes spiritual awareness of the unit of God and the immortality of the soul, as embedded in the oriental belief of reincarnation which points to belief in the futurity of life.

(c) *The floor covering:* The actual material with which the floor of any temple is finished is unimportant, but attention should be drawn to the most significant part of the floor which is made up of the square mosaic pavement, the tasselated skirt work and the letter G or the glory in the centre. These also constitute what are masonically known as the ornaments.

(d) *The roof covering:* The actual materials used for the roof covering of our temples are now insignificant and vary considerably. Whatever material is used, or whatever form it takes, however, its masonic interpretation is that it is a celestial canopy of diverse colours, even the heavens and we hope to arrive at the summit by Jacob's ladder which rests on the VSL with the three principal staves of faith, hope and charity.

(e) *The Windows:* In the VSL the windows to King Solomon's Temple are described in the following manner: 'And for the house he made windows of narrow light'. (I *Kings* 6:4).

The rituals describe the windows as the 'dormer'. In ordinary architectural parlance a dormer is a projecting upright window in a sloping roof designed to admit light to the attic as otherwise that part of the house would be without light. Masonry adopts this concept to typify that Divine Radiance without which the Holy of Holies itself would be in impenetrable darkness, and bids us lift our eyes to that source of light which reveals the hidden mysteries. The dormer is also described in our rituals as one of the ornaments of the lodge.

The windows to our temples today are designed and constructed of varying shapes, sizes and materials, but usually kept at a height that admits light in accordance with these principles, while keeping out the gaze of cowans and eavesdroppers.

(f) *The pillar/columns:* Apart from the two great pillars traditionally described as being located at the porchway or entrance to the Temple, the lodge is described as being supported by three columns which are also described as the three great pillars on which a freemason's lodge figuratively rests. These are the pillars of wisdom, strength and beauty, figuratively represented by the RWM and his Wardens. These are physically represented by the miniature columns on the pedestals of the Wardens in a regularly constituted lodge.

(g) *The porchway, the preparation room and the banquet hall:* These are necessary attachments to every regular Temple and do not require any further elaboration.

The Interior of The Temple

The interior of every regularly constituted lodge is adorned with many articles, the most important of which are grouped under Ornaments,

Furniture and Jewels. Besides these, there are other articles which have their individual merits in the working and set-up of a lodge.

(a) *The ornaments:* These are the square or mosaic pavement which is usually the centre of the lodge in its traditional colours, the indented or tasselated border which forms the skirting to the square pavement and the blazing star or letter G, which is the glory in the centre. These adorn the lodge as the main decorative features.

(b) *The furniture:* Even though every regularly constituted lodge has many articles of ordinary furniture, the only ones that are masonically regarded and recognized as the furniture of the lodge are the VSL, the square and the compasses. As we know, no lodge can be considered as being regularly opened for the commencement of working business without its furniture being appropriately displayed in the current positions.

(c) *The Jewels:* These fall into two categories, movable and immovable. The movable jewels are the square, the level and the plumb rule. The are usually attached to the pedestals of the relevant office bearers, *ie* the square on the pedestal of the RWM, the level on the pedestal of the SW and the plumb rule on the pedestal of the JW. They are also the jewels attached to the collars of office of the relevant officers and worn by them whenever a lodge is in session. They are regarded as movable jewels because they are transferred from each office holder to his successor.

The immovable jewels on the other hand are the tracing board, the rough ashlar and the perfect ashlar. These jewels are permanently displayed as components of the Temple and must not be confused with those of office which are worn by office bearers only when the lodge in session. These are discussed in a separate chapter of this book.

The Other Articles of Individual merit

Having now discussed the main group of objects under ornaments, furniture and jewels, we may now look at some of the objects of individual merit.

(a) *The lewis:* This is masonically regarded as a symbol of strength, its traditional position being at the SW corner of the Lodge, and physically represented by the implement by which the perfect ashlar is suspended — pieces of metal dovetailed into the stone and forming a clamp. The word is also usually applied masonically to the son of a mason, whose initation is permissible under the Scottish Constitution from the age of eighteen.

(b) *The greater and lesser lights:* As is generally known, the concept of light is one of the pillars in the philosophy of Masonry and in its practice the symbols of greater and lesser lights appear in every regularly constituted lodge. The greater through emblematic lights are the VSL, the square and the compasses which are conveniently situated for the purposes of the solemn obligations. The lesser lights however are displayed either at the pedestal or by the principal officers of the lodge and are meant to be on at the appropriate times.

(c) *The Charter or Warrant of constitution:* This is the instrument from which the right to constitute and hold a lodge emanates and no lodge can therefore be regularly constituted or opened without the Charter or Warrant of the constitution being present.

It is usually granted by the Grand Master in England and other countries which practise under the constitution of England, but issued by the Grand Lodge under the Scottish and the American systems. It is usually conspicuously displayed at the southeast corner of the lodge or placed in the east on the Master's pedestal. It is customarily the duty of every Master to hand it over to his successor, pure and unsullied as he received it at his installation. The practice of the issue of the charter dates from the revival of Masonry in 1717. Once issued the Charter remains in force at the pleasure of the Granter, *ie* the Grand Master or Grand Lodge, until it is revoked. If it is destroyed or misplaced it must be recovered or another granted in substitution, before the lodge can be convened or opened for any regular business.

(d) *The Ashlars* (rough or perfect): An Ashlar is a square hewn stone or freestone as it comes out of the quarry. Being based on the science of building, Masonry speculatively adopts this as representing man and his character. Accordingly, every lodge has two ashlars; the 'rough ashlar', traditionally located at the NE corner of the Lodge, and the 'perfect ashlar', traditionally at the SW corner, and constituting the lewis.

The rough ashlar, in its natural unpolished form in the NE corner where the initiate is given his NE charge at Initiation, is emblematic of man in his natural state — ignorant, uncultivated, vicious, rough and unpolished in relation to the tenets of Freemasonry. When by his Initiation he is assisted under the skilful hands of workmen to be smoothed and squared, and when by education and the extension of his researches into more hidden mysteries his passions are restrained to the extend that he achieves that purity of life and action, then he becomes the perfect ashlar, fitted for the building of the moral temple.

(e) *The Pedestals:* Every regularly constituted lodge is supported by three columns which symbolically represent wisdom, strength and beauty, and these are in turn represented by the RWM, the SW and the JW, since the columns cannot be erected in the lodge. A pedestal being the base of a column on which the shaft is placed, the positions of the RWM, the SW and the JW are known as pedestals. There are therefore three pedestals in a regularly constituted lodge: the RWM in the east, the SW in the west and JW in the south.

A fourth, general pedestal, sometimes called the altar on which the VSL, the square and compass rest, and at which all solemn obligations are taken, is usually sited in the centre of the lodge at the mosaic pavement.

Office Bearers and Brethrens as Parts of the Lodge

Having considered the physical items and components of the lodge it may be necessary to consider the office bearers and brethren as parts of the lodge, as their official locations are not generally known to young masons. But since the detailed outlines of their stations would not be appropriate in a volume of this nature, the mason is here merely invited to observe the positions of:

1. The Right Worshipful Master
2. The Senior Warden
3. The Junior Warden
4. The Deputy Master
5. The Immediate Past Master
6. The Substitute Master
7. The Senior Deacon
8. The Junior Deacon
9. The Chaplain
10. The Secretary
11. The Treasurer
12. The Inner Guard
13. The Outer Guard, or Tyler
14. The Past Masters of the Lodge
15. Visiting Past Masters

16. District Grand, and Grand Lodge Office Bearers
17. The Entered Apprentices
18. The Fellow Crafts
19. The Master Masons

This observation is invited because the traditional positions of the office bearers and body of masons have become so customary that they constitute a part of the temple once the lodge is in session. In order that a candidate may belong fully, he ought truly to know these things.

10

MASONRY, RELIGION, CHRISTIANITY AND THE CHURCH

There is no religion higher than 'truth' and it is dogma alone, the brainchild of most religions, that stifles primeval truth, for the spirit whose essence is eternal, one and self existent emanates a pure ethereal light not circumscribable by dogma or creed, and sanctified by the orthodox traditional idea of our Deity common to Christianity, Islam, Judaism and all religions — the reverent awareness of His Being.

A MAJORITY OF freemasons embrace the religion of the Christian faith and more particularly the Church of England, otherwise known as the Anglican Church. Substantial numbers also belong to the other Protestant denominations and some are Roman Catholics. When a person is both mason and Christian, he has almost invariably been a Christian before admission to Masonry and the majority of such masons keep both to the end of their lives.

At the point of admission, both are in a state of ignorance, the Christian usually during his biological childhood, the mason in his spiritual childhood. They are equally ignorant, for what can a child know of the Christian faith to which he is being admitted through baptism? No more than the mason knows about Masonry at his Initiation.

It is a recognized fact that one of the greatest honours in a masonic career in England is to be appointed a Prestonian lecturer. Between 1925 and 1974 seven of the 44 Prestonian lecturers have been men of high ecclesiastical status as the list demonstrates:

1931 *Medieval Master Masons and their Secrets*, The Rev Canon W. W. Covey-Crump

1933 *The Old Charges in 18th Century Masonry*, The Rev Herbert Poole

1937 *The Inwardness of Masonic Symbolism*, The Rev Joseph Johnson
1959 *The Medieval Organisation of Freemason Lodges*, The Rev Canon J. S. Purvis
1963 *Folklore into Masonry*, The Rev H. G. Michael Clark
1971 *Masters and Master Masons*, The Rev Canon R. Tydeman
1974 *Drama and the Craft*, The Rev Neville B. Cryer

Records show that very many distinguished masons have been men of high ecclesiastical calling and status. Lord Fisher, who was Grand Chaplain in 1937 and 1939, was Archbishop of Canterbury from 1945-61. The Rt Rev Dr Percy M. Herbert, former Bishop of Norwich, was a mason. The Most Rev A. Aboyade-Cole, Primate of the African Church (Inc), was District Chaplain, Nigeria. The Rt Rev Dr Edward Sydney (1878-1953), Bishop of Lichfield, was a mason. The Most Rev Okusanya was PM Lodge Faith 1271 SC and Superintendent General of WA, UNA Churches. The Very Rev Sir Israel Brodie rose to the rank of Grand Chaplain. Dr Rev Major Okon Asuquo Inyang held the post of District Grand Chaplain (Nigeria) for many years, and Most Rev Archbishop George Kingston (1889-1950) was a mason and Primate of Canada (1947-50).

It would be idle to continue a catalogue of personalities who are both distinguished masons and ecclesiastics, as such a list would serve only for reference. There would appear therefore to be a common bond between Freemasonry and the Christian religion, but it is on record that, since the first quarter of the 18th century, Masonry as an institution has been under attack by certain Christian religious bodies, more especially the Papal See, to such an extent that the question has even been asked, *Should a Christian be a Freemason*? A corollary to this has been the enormous amount of time and energy spent in determining whether Masonry is a religion or not, and earlier efforts by masonic scholars and writers to prove that it is not. Thus, an apparent conflict has been created and sustained over the relationship between masonry, Christianity, religion and the Church. Conflicts between doctrines or philosophies are often caused by different levels of understanding of their real substance. Conflicts in the interpretation of a particular doctrine have often been caused in the same way, for example the conflicting interpretations of the Christian doctrine of the 'Virgin birth' and 'Resurrection', both central to the fabric of the Christian faith.

Similarly, in this case it is clear to any serious thinker that the apparent conflict between Masonry and Christianity can only be a result of a very shallow understanding of the real substance in Freemasonry, religion and Christianity, or a selfish desire for self-

Plate E: *Revd Supt Okunsanya, PM.*

protection (particularly on the part of the Church) which borders on calumny.

What therefore, is the real substance in Freemasonry, and how does it compare with the substance in religion and Christianity?

The total substance of Freemasonry, or its real meaning is expressed in three words: faith, hope and charity manifesting in total human and spiritual fulfilment for all who understand. When expanded, the three words would mean faith in the Unity, universality and Fatherhood of a Supreme Being who is the ruler of the universe, hope in the immortality of the soul or the futurity of life and charity in the brotherhood of man, expressed in love. All others are ritualistic, allegorical and symbolic appendages, or rules of conduct which are supportive of the main substance and at the same time aiding our understanding.

Similarly, the main substance of Christianity is three-fold: a belief in the unity of God as Supreme Ruler, hope in the futurity of life as expressed in the hope for resurrection, and love for your neighbours as yourself. All others are creeds, doctrines, catechisms and rituals which by their nature are sectarian, and thus create unwholesome divisions even between sectors of the Christian faith. The emphasis placed on these creeds, doctrines and rituals as against the substance of religion, has created differences in the Christian, Hindu, Muslim and other religions of the world. From the foregoing the real substance of Freemasonry would appear to be the same as that of the Christian faith, except for the Christian sectarian creeds and doctrines which, though superficial, have been so accepted by the Church with such authoritative dogma for its own self-protection, that reconciliation between one denomination and another has become a problem, though they all profess to worship the same God. Let a man's religion be what it is.

Masonic thought is devoid of sectarian creeds and adopts the main substance which runs through all religions to the extent that the Christian, Muslim, Hindu, Jew, etc find a common heritage in elevating mutual worship. For this reason, Masonry is described as not being a religion, as it absorbs all religions except paganism and is manifestly religious in character. It is only in this sense that it can be described as not being a religion. 'The first condition of admission into, and membership of, the Order is belief in the Supreme Being. This is essential and admits to no compromise. Thereafter let a man's religion or mode of worship be what it may, he is not excluded from the Order provided he believes in the glorious Architect of Heaven and earth, and practices the sacred duties of morality.' (*Aims and Relationships of the Craft.*)

Accordingly, the epithet 'free' has now been generally accepted to mean that every brother is free to practice his religion. There is no religion higher than truth and it is dogma alone, the brainchild of most religions, which has for so long stifled primeval truth; Masonry does not concern itself with sectarian dogma. No human-born doctrine, no creed however sanctified by custom and antiquity, can compare in sacredness with the religion of nature. The keys of wisdom that unlock the massive gates that lead to the sanctuaries can be found hidden in her bosom and that is what Masonry is about.

Indeed, wherever prominence is given to orthodoxy and doctrine, anything outside the normal is regarded as the work of the devil, superstition or sacrilege. This is the fallacy of the Vatican. The spirit whose essence is eternal, one and self-existent emanates a pure ethereal light — not circumscribable by dogma or creed, and common in the Purana, in the Bible, in the Sepher Jezirah, the Greek and Latin hymns, the book of Hermes, the Chaldean Book of Humbers, the esoterism of Lao-Tse, Kabala, Bagavit Gita, everywhere. This is the source that poets and musicians through pure inspiration are able to tap and what makes the language of poetry and music universal and completely devoid of sectarianism, and the science of Freemasonry universal.

The Attitude of the Church

Even though Masonry has never attacked Roman Catholicism or Christianity in general, and has no need to do so, acts of hostility have been levelled against the Order from time to time. The first act of hostility in 1738 was the famous Bull of Pope Clement XII, *In Emenenti Apostolatus Specula*. Hostilities were renewed on 18 May 1751, with the Bull *Providas* of Pope Benedict XIV. Then followed the edict of Pius VII on 13 September 1821, prohibiting participation in meetings of Freemasons. The next major move was the prohibition of all secret societies for ever by Leo XII in the Apostolic edict *Quo Graviora* of 13 March 1825. The attack continued through several papal reigns with edicts by Pius VIII on 21 May 1829, Gregory XVI on 15 August 1832, Pius IX in 1846. Leo XVIII who ascended the papal throne in 1878 issued his Bull or Encyclical Letter *Humanum Genus* on 20 April 1884. This Bull, while accepting that Freemasonry as a society is widespread and well established, served as confirmation and ratification of all the previous ones. This hostile attitude continued until the ecumenical reign of Pope John XXIII (1958-63) which saw a thawing of the Catholic attitude toward the regular Grand Lodges. Becoming a Freemason was a breach of these Bulls and the sanction was excommunication involving the withdrawal of all spiritual privileges while living and the rites of burial when dead.

The attack does not seem to have been limited to the Roman Catholic Church. At the pastoral session of the Methodist Conference in 1927, a vigorous attack was launched on the Order led by the Rev C. Penny Hunt, which proved a slip. It was revived in an article in *Theology* in 1951, entitled 'Should a Christian be a Freemason?' by the Rev Walton Hannah. He drew references of what he considered to be Masonry's gnostic nature from similar and earlier attacks by the Roman Catholics and Methodists. The discussions which followed during the June Assembly of the Church in annual session are now matters of history relating to the motion tabled by the Rev R. Creed Meredith. The contributions made by eminent ecclesiastics such as the Rev K. Healey, the Rev C. Douglas, the Archbishop of York, are also known. Mr Hannah has of course pursued the matter further by publishing his book *Darkness Visible* which is an analytical attempt at comparing Christianity and Freemasonry.

The persecution of Freemasonry has not been confined to these Christian bodies alone. In 1957 the associate synod of seceders of Scotland adopted an Act concerning what they called 'The Mason Oath', in which it is declared that all persons who shall refuse to make such revelations as the Kirk Session may require, and to promise to abstain from all connections with the Order 'shall be reputed under scandal and incapable of admission to sealing ordnances' or as earlier expressed by Pope Clement, 'be *ibso facto* excommunicated'.

In the preamble to the Act, the Synod listed certain reasons for their objection to the Order, and the ecclesiastical censure of all who contract it. 'That there were strong presumptions that among Masons an oath of secrecy is administered to entrants into the Society even under a capital penalty and before any of those things which they swear to keep secret be revealed to them, and that they pretend to take some of these secrets from the Bible, besides other things which are grounds of scruple in the manner of swearing such oath.'

Experience has shown that in West Africa, for example, there was considerable harmony between the Church and Masonry, except the Roman Catholic Church up to the early 1970s when hostility in the usual manner started, probably triggered off by the growth of Freemasonry which was erroneously considered a threat.

Reasons for the Attack

Some reasons for the hostility are contained in the encyclical letter *Humanum Genus* of April 1884:

(a) That the human race after its most miserable defection from its creator God, the giver of celestial gifts, has divided into two opposite and different factions. One fights for truth and virtue, the other for the opposites. One is the Kingdom of God on earth, and the other is the kingdom of Satan. This in general religious terms is what is described as the fall of man and in masonic terms the death of our Master in the celebrated allegory.

(b) That Masonry admits men of all religions, and that in accepting all that present themselves, no matter of what religion, Masonry urges that the question of religion should be left undetermined and that there should be no distinction made between varieties.

(c) That this policy aims at the destruction of all religions, especially the Catholic religion, which since it is the only true one cannot be reduced to equality with the rest without the greatest injury.

(d) That Masonry is a secret society and is practiced in secret.

(e) That the nature of the oaths and obligations taken on the VSL are barbaric, satanic, unchristian and irreligious.

(f) That by not mentioning Jesus in its deliberations, Masonry does not believe in the triune essence of God and is therefore unchristian.

It is gratifying to note that in spite of these Bulls there were men not only of courage but of inner understanding who defied them as Catholics. Thomas Matthew was privately installed as Grand Master in 1767, Robert Edward, 9th Lord Petre who was looked upon as head of the Catholic Community in England, held office as Grand Master after the Papal denunciations of 1738 and 1751.

The Search for Understanding

It has already been stated that the main substance of both Freemasonry and Christianity — or indeed any other religion except paganism — is faith in the unity and universality of a Supreme Being, God. This faith has kept men throughout history searching for understanding, and this search has caused various concepts of God to be developed, resulting in various doctrines and creeds. The criticisms of Freemasonry by the Church can only be examined against this background.

There is the orthodox traditional idea of God common to Christianity, Islam, Judaism, Masonry and all religions, which is the reverent awareness of His Being as it truly is. This is basically shared by Aquinas, Maimonides and Al-Ghazali, the major philosophers of the Christian, Jewish and Muslim faiths. God is an infinite and eternally Divine reality and man throughout history has continuously striven to

Plate F: *Robert Edward, 9th Lord Petre.*

relate to Him through the accessible medium of finite things of time and space, comprehensible to him since the God essence which is Divine is incomprehensible even though we are reverently aware. In this way, and from time immemorial, man has approached his God in various ways — by signs, sacrifices, prostrations, special apparels and regalia, ornaments, symbols, fasting, rituals and words. There are common to Masonry as they are to Christianity — baptism, pectoral cross, Eucharist, etc.

Because God is incomprehensible, man has striven to relate to him sometimes through history and at other times through legend and allegory. This has given rise to belief in the incarnation of certain elements of His Essence in Jesus of Nazareth by the Christians, Abdru Shin by the Cross Bearers, Olumba, Olumba Obu, by the Brotherhood of the Cross and Star, etc, because man's belief tends to find reality when anchored in historical or physical facts limited in time and space, which the human mind can comprehend. This element in man is also assisted by the fact that he is material and spiritual, so internal and external, corporal and psychic, gross material and ethereal, limited yet reaching for the unlimited. In the great quest for understanding, theology places the deluge at 2,448 BC and the creation of the world only at 5,890 years ago. The geologists and physicists estimate the age of our globe as 10m to 1,000m years, while the anthropologists place the appearance of man on the globe between 25,000 and 500,000 years ago. The differences in these estimates appear to be striking, but what matters is not the differences but the quest to understand and know.

The Bible, which is the Holy Writ on which Christianity rests, bears testimony to man's perpetual struggle to relate to his God, and his tendency sometimes to regard Him as a tribal God. The natural and passionate impulse among every race was to exalt its own deity above all others, and even the chosen people from whom Christianity sprang regarded God as the God of the Israelites, no more than a 'tribal God'. Indeed, the Bible records that God appeared to Abraham and said 'I am the Almighty God. I will establish my covenant to be a God unto thee' (*Gen* XVII:7) implying that he was not God of other races. Moses is said to have found reality in God through His revelation in the burning bush and the qualification of not only 'I am that I am' but 'the God of Abraham the God of Isaac and the God of Jacob' (*Exodus* 3.4:6) thus circumscribing God in a relationship of historically and physically finite terms. This may of course be said to mean that God manifests Himself only to minds that are prepared for His reception.

The Israelites even found reality in the direct intervention of their God for the purposes of their exodus through the plagues, the river of blood and even the death of the first sons of the Egyptians (*Exodus* 7-12). In the songs of Moses the Lord is even described as a man of war (*Exodus* 15:3).

Indeed in man's search for the fuller and richer truth cradled in nature's bosom, he has attempted to reach God physically through the Tower of Babel, while the prophets have compared Him with images of a woman in travail (*Isaiah* 42) or a breast-feeding mother (*Isaiah* 49).

Covenants, Oaths and Penalties

Man's continuous search for a meaningful relationship with God has also found expression in his acceptance of the covenants, oaths, rituals and penalties that have guided his being and mode of worship, because covenants and oaths have always formed the foundation of loyalties of all kinds. Covenants and oaths have almost always been attendant with ceremonies and solemnity in rituals. In general, rituals are meant to condition the state of the participant over time to be transported mentally and spiritually, and any break of familiarity breaks the circle. This is why changes and innovations are undesirable, slow, if they do take place, and described in Freemasonry as 'not in the power of any man or body of men'.

Penalties on the other hand are elements for the regulation of society. When imposed by governments, they are regarded as sanctions and have even been as crude as the forcible taking of human life. They are also indicative of spiritual preparedness for the objectives of oaths or covenants when taken subjectively. The Biblical rewards of Heaven and Hell and the penalties of wailing and gnashing of teeth, believed to be imposed by God himself, reveal man's understanding of his God through antiquity. Abraham even acceded to the request for the sacrifice of his son Isaac as burnt offering for God. The Bible contains, in *Gen* 15, the first record of covenants in the scriptures in the custom of the Hebrews. Abraham in obedience to the Divine command took a heifer, a she-goat and a ram 'and divided them in the midst and laid each piece, one against the other' (*Gen* 15:10).

In Jeremiah, the penalty for violation of the covenant is expressed as follows: 'I will even give them [ie the violators] into the hands of their enemies and into the hands of them that seek their life, and their dead bodies shall be for meat unto the fowls of the heavens and to the beasts of the earth' (*Jeremiah* XXXIV 18, 19, 20). We may also observe these passages that appear in the Bible.

'Now this is that which thou shalt offer upon the altar, two lambs of the first year day by day continually' (*Ex* 29: 38) 'And with the one lamb, a tenth deal of flour mingled with the fourth of an hin of beaten oil, and the fourth part of an hin of wine for a drink offering' (*Ex* 29: 40). The pagan nature of these rituals does not make the Bible any less the Holy Writ on which the Christian doctrine is based, since it is realised (or ought to be) that these practices were either mere ritual drama, or allegorical or a revelation of man's understanding of his God at that time and his desire to relate to Him. Rituals are a means to an end and not the end in themselves. The Christian faith is rich in rituals — the Last Supper, Holy Communion, Baptism, Eucharist, the Mass, etc are available in the *Book of Common Prayer* or *Ordinal for the Roman Church* and constitute the structure of the Church.

Has Masonry Maintained Harmony with Religion and Christianity?

While Masonry is eminently religious in nature it does not meddle in sectarian creeds and doctrines, for it believes that the universal truth transcends sectarianism in nature. Christianity, on the other hand, places emphasis on form which is superficial. Thus a man may be truly religious without being a mason, but no man can be a mason without being religious.

Indeed, until two centuries ago, candidates for Freemsonry, especially in the United Kingdom, were required to be of a Christian religion and to declare a specific belief in the Trinity. Following the union in 1813, Masonry ceased to be a Christian Order. So long as the candidate believes in God he is free to practice his religion and to interpret his symbols, allegories, etc according to his spiritual understanding through revelation, faith in the sacred writings in the VSL, level steps and square conduct.

The 'Sacred Truths' that constitute the total substance of Freemasonry are of antiquity and were there at the beginning when 'The Word was with God, and the Word was God'. They were in existence before the incarnation of any part of our Deity and are therefore older than Christianity. The Bible bears eloquent testimony to this in *St Matthew* 5.17: 'Think not that I am come to destroy the law or the prophets; I am not come to destroy but to fulfil'. Christian creeds have very often tended to becloud this very illuminating passage which has led to the controversy between the conservative evangelists and evangelical liberalism, which also shows what doctrines can do to split believers. The recent attempts made by Dr Runcie, then the Archbishop of Canterbury, to distinguish between primary and secondary matters of doctrine is a pointer to the irritating circumstances created by the views of evangelical liberalism in serious matters of doctrine such as the Virgin Birth and the Resurrection. Perhaps Christianity would retain more strength if it tried to distinguish between history and ritual drama in the life and history of Christ in relation to his death and resurrection.

The Criticism

(a) *The Triune Essence of God*

The main controversy, though merely apparent between Christianity and Masonry, is in the doctrines and beliefs concerning the triune nature of our Deity and especially in relation to the life and death of Jesus. This again is attributable to shallowness of understanding of the critics of Masonry. It is not in the nature of our science to sustain disharmony, but we also have an obligation to be cautious and the explanations that follow are guided by these principles. Besides, it is realised that wherever some messenger of light proclaimed the truth according to the will of God, he was attacked, defiled and persecuted. These attacks and persecutions were almost invariably carried out by representatives of established religious dogma, who professed to be keepers of the Divine Will. The primitive medicine man, the sorcerer and even the highest prophets have always felt themselves menaced by the Truth and have resorted to veiled agitation or even open mischief of the sort contained in the ecumenical letter referred to earlier in this chapter. In other words by virtue of the transcendency of the truths contained in masonic philosophy the church finds herself thereatened.

Masonry is a progressive science and the relationship between it and the son of God Himself is found only in the 'higher' degrees, while Craft Masonry dwells on the sacred truths embodied in the laws that it was the purpose of the son of God to fulfil.

The ancient manuscripts on Freemasonry otherwise known as the *Old Constitutions* are the 'title deeds' of Masonry, providing the historical framework of the laws, regulations, customs and usage that govern the Order. They bear eloquent testimony of the historical relationship between Freemasonry and Christianity.

The Halliwel or Regius Poem

This was the earliest manuscript dating from 1390. It is definitely Catholic in character and was in all probability written by a Catholic priest who was a Mason. The document opens with an invocation to the Trinity and the Virgin Mary. Freemasons were loyal churchmen and remained so throughout the golden age of the minsters and cathedrals.

The Antiquity Ms 1686 AD

This manuscript opens with the following:

> 'Fear God and Keep His commandments, for this is
> the whole duty of man.
> 'In the name of the Great and Holy God,
> The wisdom of the son and the goodness
> of the holy Ghost, three persons and one,
> God be with us now and ever.
> Amen'

The Harleian Ms rev 1942 (M) about 1679

This manuscript bears the following wording:

> 'The Almighty Father of Heaven, with the wisdome
> of the glorious sonne, through the goodness of
> the Holy Ghost, three persons in one Godhead,
> bee with our beginning and give us grace soe
> to governe our lives that we may come to his
> bliss that never shall have end.
> Amen'

These two passages contain not only the concept of the triune essence of our Deity but also the concept of the immortality of the soul. Above all, the groundwork of our laws may be found in *Andersons Constitutions*, 1723. Anderson was a Presbyterian minister in charge of the Presbyterian chapel in Swallow Street, Piccadilly, London until 1734 and chaplain to the Earl of Buchan, 1714-34.

So we see that Masonry has grown historically from having affinities with the Catholic, then the Protestant Church after the Reformation, and non-denominational after the Anderson constitution. Indeed, even at the present day, no lodge can be properly constituted for the purposes of any transaction without the Volume of the Sacred Law being open on the Pedestal as the symbol of faith in the unity and will of God.

Many respected masonic writers, including Hutchinson and Oliver, have tried to interpret some of the symbols and traditions as having a Christian base. The whole structure of the Order is based on the allegory of the building of King Solomon's Temple, while the ceremony of masonic manhood at the third degree is based on the immortality of the soul and the resurrection of the body. This is so, even though it is known that Masonry is older than Christianity. Doctrines related to the continuity of life after physical death were known to several communities before Christ, that is, before Christianity.

Masonic practice is replete with symbolism related to the triune nature of our Deity. As early as 200 years ago, the three knocks of

Bro Tyler and at all 1° workings were taken as referring to the Trinity; similarly the triune essence of the Deity was symbolised by the three great lights in the centre of the floor of the Lodge, in the form of a triangle. The triune essence of our Deity is expressed in Christian terms as God the Father, God the Son and God the Holy Ghost. At the same time, God the Son represents the essence of Love while God the Holy Ghost represents the essence of His Will.

In the same manner masons know and are admonished in Masonry that the VSL is symbolically representative of faith in the unity of God the Father, the square is representative of the regulation of our actions which is love, and the compasses of keeping us in due bounds with all mankind, which is keeping His laws, which is the same as His Will. The three great though emblematical lights in Masonry therefore represent the essence of His Fatherhood, His Love and His Will. The triune essence of our Deity is therefore acknowledged to have the same components in both Christianity and Masonry.

The three knocks were also taken in the old lectures to be symbolic spiritually of one of the great admonitions in the Bible: 'Seek and ye shall find, ask and ye shall receive, knock and it shall be opened unto you' (*Luke* 11: 9). This passage also re-emphasises the desire of Masons to protect the value of their secrets, reserving them for minds that both desire and are prepared for them.

The closing ceremony in the 2° of Craft Masonry bears further eloquent testimony, for the sacred symbol which is situated in the centre of the building is said to be in the form of a triangle. Being a symbol of spiritual perfection, the triangle can only relate to God as implied in His triune nature. If therefore the tenets and principles practiced by Freemasonry are the same as those the Son of God came to fulfil, then the two institutions cannot be seen to be opposed to one another.

It is clear to me that belief in the Son of God has a deeper meaning than the incarnation, birth and resurrection of the body. It is for this reason that the Bible teaches *Not everyone that saith unto me, Lord, Lord, shall enter into the Kingdom of Heaven, but he that doeth the will of my Father* (*St Matthew* 7: 21) and that is what Craft Masonry is about.

(b) *Practice and Secrecy*

The reasons for the protection of the values of the Order in secrecy have been stated elsewhere and need no repetition here. Freemasonry is not a secret society but, even if it were, the tenets and principles practiced by the Order are so elevating that no one need be ashamed of them. Nature herself, although described as an open book, enshrouds her values in secrecy, as has been stated elsewhere in this book. In relation to the Christian faith, mention has already been made of the

Plate G: *Milan Cathedral.*

Conclave of Bishops, the traditions of the Vatican, the administration of Holy Communion, the Mass or Eucharist, the Knights of Saint Columba (of Columbus in USA) etc, but above all there is the injunction in the Bible 'Give not that which is Holy unto the dogs, neither cast ye your pearls before swine lest they trample them under their feet, and turn again and rend you' (*St Matthew* 7: 6).

(c) *The Nature of the Oaths*

The nature and object of oaths generally, whether masonic, Christian or lay, have been discussed and need no repetition here. The masonic oaths should be examined against the background of the ancient nature of the Order, the symbolic base of its overall structure and man's continuous attempts to relate to his Creator in terms similar to those stated in the volume of the Sacred Law, where the procedure for the performance of certain covenants coincides with the penalties of the 1st, 2nd and 3rd degrees in Craft Masonry. The apparent coincidence of these oaths between the Bible and Masonry can only be related to a continuing search for the recognition of God. Even against the background of antiquity and the symbolic nature of the penalties in the obligations, modifications have been made by all three constitutions (in some cases permissively, in others compulsorily) in response to the concern expressed among masons as a result of their growing awareness.

Oaths generally are an undertaking of allegiance to a person or persons, or a course of conduct, and it is therefore reasonable to expect that they should come before the course of conduct. This is so in the case of monarchs, heads of state or government, popes and bishops, parliamentarians, masons, heads of the judiciary or indeed any post demanding some measure of responsibility.

The relationship between Masonry and religion has been asserted by the Grand Lodge in 1961: 'Masonry is neither a religion nor a substitute for it. Believe in a Supreme Being and practice your religion'. The confederation of peoples from all religions and sects into a mysterious bond of union is based on eternal truths which transcend sectarian creeds and doctrines, for the human spirit in pure understanding and pure love is above circumscription by creeds and doctrines. It is this that will sustain Freemasonry through all vicissitudes.

11

IN DEFENCE OF SECRECY

His language is the influence of a higher light through which the spirit which He pervades becomes electrified and when by this process He reveals Himself through our perceptive intuition, then it is described as the still small voice of calm.

MASONRY IS NOT a secret society, as has been stated. Secrecy and silence are the virtues which constitute the very essence of the masonic character, lending to the Order both security and perpetuity and candidates are so admonished in all the degrees. The Entered Apprentice begins his career by learning the useful lessons of secrecy and silence while even in the 9th or Select Masters Degree of the American rite, secrecy and silence are described as 'the cardinal virtues of a Select Master'.

God speaks to us not in so many words but silently in His creation, which is an open book and yet enshrouded in secrecy. His language is the influence of a higher light through which the Spirit which He pervades becomes electrified, and when by this process He reveals Himself through our perceptive intuition, then it is described as 'the still small voice of calm'. God acts as a centrum only on the centrum of things, *ie* on the inner or spiritual. The outward manifestations follow thereafter.

It has been a recognized phenomenon that much talking inhibits man's purer capacity to perceive intuitively, and creates the alternative effect of loss of confidence among associates, even when the talking is seemingly harmless. If Masonry claims to be an institution which helps in the development of our perceptive intuition, then silence and secrecy must of necessity be essential ingredients of the Order. But maintaining silence and secrecy does not necessarily make an organization into a secret society. If it does, then there would be hardly any organization or relationship which would not qualify as a secret society.

The ancient Egyptians had so great a regard for secrecy and silence in the mysteries of their religion that they set up the god Harpocrates who was represented with his right hand placed near his heart, and the left down by his side, covered with a skin full of eyes and ears to signify that, of many things to be seen and heard, few are to be published. Aristotle, when asked what appeared to him most difficult of performance, replied 'To be secret and silent'.

'By no peril will I be compelled to disclose to the uninitiated the things that I have had entrusted to me on condition of silence.' This was the declaration of Apuleius, an initiate into the mysteries of Isis. In the school of Pythagoras these lessons were taught by the sage to his disciples with a novitiate of five years of total silence passed in religious and philosophical contemplation, at the end of which an oath was administered for the preservation of the lessons.

In African mythology silence was indicated by pressing the palm against the lips with the thumb outstretched in the form of a square, while among the Egyptians the sign was made by pressing the index finger of the right hand on the lips. Masons are taught to be cautious in their speech and to guard their words, because the order realises the potency of human words as being equal to deeds, as they do in fact take form in the plane of fine gross matter and consequently affect everything earthly. We are therefore not to squander these sublime gifts which the Great Architect of the Universe has so mercifully granted us. It is in this regard that the Holy Writ admonishes: 'Let your yea be yea and your nay be nay' for our words may hold joy or sorrow for us, they may build or disintegrate, they may bring clarity or even cause confusion, according to the manner spoken and applied. We must therefore at all times strive to maintain purity in our words by keeping them simple and true.

'This is my beloved son in whom I am well pleased, hear ye him'. This was God's injunction to the disciples Peter, James and John at the transfiguration of the Son of God at Mount Hermon as recorded in the Holy Writ. This was followed by the vision in which the disciples saw Moses and Elias. The antecedent injunction from the Son of God was 'Tell the vision to no man until the son of man be risen again from the dead'. (*Matthew* 17:1-10).

The Son of God started preparation for his ministry with 40 days and nights of solitude and silence for spiritual strength. Moses in his ecstatic second sight foresaw that he would prepare the children of Israel for the pure worship of God and guard them against error and idolatry, only by isolating them in the wilderness.

From time immemorial and even among His chosen people, God's communication with His prophets and men consecrated to Him is generally in the solitude of dreams and visions. 'In a dream, in a vision at night when deep sleep falleth upon men in slumberings upon the bed, then He openeth the ears of men and sealeth their instructions' (I *Kings* 111:5).

What Therefore is a Secret Society?

The term 'secret society' is nebulous. It is a socio-political concept and therefore varies in content and definition from one entity to another. Accordingly, what is a secret society in the United Kingdom may be completely different from what it was in the USSR, and thus there is no such thing as a secret society universally known to all communities; its meaning if any is relevant only to the socio-political entity that defines it.

The dictionary interpretation of a secret society is 'a society whose members are sworn to secrecy about it.' In general terms, secret societies may be of two kinds:

(a) Those which may maintain secrecy regarding their modes of recognition and doctrine, and in addition in relation to the objects of the association, times and places of meetings and even the record of membership. In this category may be included some societies which sprang up in the Middle Ages, such as the Vehn Gericht of Westphalia formed for the secret punishment of criminals, and in the 18th century political societies such as the 'Carbonari' organized for resistance to despotism or tyrannical governments.

(b) Those whose secrets are in the method of their recognition, certain symbols and doctrines and methods of instruction which are obtained only after initiation and with a promise not to part with them unless . . . To this belong all the moral or religious associations of antiquity, the ancient mystery orders, schools of philosophers such as Plato and Pythagoras who distinguished between esoterism of doctrines and exoteric communication to scholars. Such is Freemasonry and the so-called modern secret societies.

Indeed, after the French Revolution a number of laws designed to prevent seditious practices were passed, the culmination of which was the *Statute 39 George III c.79* commonly known as 'the Unlawful Societies Act of 1779'. This Act made illegal all societies whose members were bound by a secret oath and yet Freemasons' lodges were especially exempt provided a list of lodge members, with other details, was returned to the Clerk of the Peace annually.

This act is believed to have been substantially influenced by the publications of Abbe Barruel and Prof Robinson in 1779. Both falsely

Plate H: *The three Constitutions in defence of our faith.*

and mischievously sought to prove that a secret society had been formed and operated with a view to rooting out all existing governments in Europe, and that this association had employed as its chief instrument the lodges of freemasons. Barruel and Prof Johnson thus made the mistake of classifying Freemasonry under the first category, which it is not, and consequently even if the first state prohibition were to include Freemasonry, the inclusion would have been influenced by falsehood.

Does the maintenance of secrecy in Freemasonry offend the accepted norms of civilised society?

Man's total being finds expression in relation to one or a combination of three elements constituting the motivating circumstances of his existence in his day-to-day environment:

(a) his motivation by natural circumstances;

(b) his motivation by socio-economic circumstances; and

(c) his motivation by religious and spiritual circumstances.

Whenever man errs or offends by his actions, he must do so against the accepted norms of any of these circumstances and his condemnation must also be in accordance with the norms of these circumstances. If Masonry is found to be offensive because of its secrecy, then it must be examined against the background of these circumstances, to determine whether or not secrecy is within the norms generally allowable by these circumstances in other directions. Accordingly it may be asked '*How does society generally react to secrecy in relation to any of the aforementioned circumstances?*' In general, the protection of things of esteem has been a common characteristic in society from time immemorial and therefore not peculiar to Masonry. The strictness of the protection is a measure of the esteem that attaches to what is being protected.

It is common knowledge, though not easily discernible, that the protection of vital elements in order to maintain their inherent beauty and esteem is an attribute of nature from which man derives his motivation under the natural circumstances of his existence. He is even described as being made in the image of God. Nature itself is an open book but yet is enshrined in secrecy for the purpose of protection of certain vital elements contained in His creation unless they are revealed to us by the acquisition of knowledge and wisdom. Protein, a class of organic compound important in all living organisms, is unseen to the naked eye but present in the meat we eat. Vitamins, vital for normal growth and nutrition, are equally hidden in the food we eat.

Air, the most vital element for our existence, is unseen, unfelt, untouched and designed by nature to be so. Gold, crude oil, silver, etc are all hidden in their natural states until discovered by a trained mind. Even in the allegory of Adam and Eve in the Bible, whose sacred writings are to guide our faith, the tree of knowledge and the tree of life were to be protected until Adam and Eve were prepared for their reception and participation. These principles of nature are again clearly illustrated in the great admonition in the volume of the sacred law — seek and ye shall find, ask and ye shall receive, knock and it shall be opened unto you.

In a similar manner, man's socio-economic circumstances are replete with examples of acceptable norms of secrecy. It is accepted that most professionals such as lawyers, architects, surveyors, doctors, engineers, etc practice only after long preparation and readiness, and keep the practice select and protected from profanity with support extending to legal sanctions.

In commercial practice incorporated bodies keep their minutes and deliberations secret, while the process of incorporation which could be ascertained from the Registrar of Companies is public knowledge. Patent registration is made an acceptable norm for the protection of the secrecy of new inventions.

In the process of administration of governments, heads of state and government, members of the judiciary, of the House of Lords, prime ministers, monarchs and others of such levels of responsibility are enjoined by their oath of office to maintain a strict level of secrecy in order that the system is preserved. Members who are appointed to tribunals, court martials and bodies of similar responsibility are bound to secrecy by a sworn obligation as secrecy is essential in conducting worldly affairs and such sworn obligations are described severally as oaths of office, covenants, oaths of allegiance, solemn promise, solemn obligation, etc.

Government secrets are usually very vigorously protected by official secrets acts. In Britain, for example. Section 2 of the *Official Secrets Act*, 1911, has always been a source of disagreement and yet it is maintained in what is glibly described as 'in the interests of the state'. The British parliament witnessed in 1985 an unprecedented furore that surrounded the Clive Ponting case and the savage acrimony between the Prime Minister and the Leader of the Opposition was all in defence of Government secrecy.

It is even on record that on 24 March 1985 Major Arthur Nicholson, an American army officer, was shot dead by a Russian guard in East Germany. The Russian Embassy in Washington alleged that Major Nicholson, 37, was caught red-handed photographing Soviet military equipment. The Major was said to have entered a restricted military area in Schwerin. *Murder was clearly committed in defence of secrecy, here described as security.*

From the standpoint of man's religious and spiritual motivation, the value of secrecy and silence has already been discussed. It is significant that there are several accepted norms of secrecy existing in all religions and mystery orders and these are discoverable in their rituals, doctrines, practices and customs. The Conclave of Bishops in Christian religious orders is kept secret and exclusive. Holy Communion is administered only to those who by preparation are qualified for it in accordance with the custom of the Christian faith. Each hierarchy is thus at all times limited to a level that is prepared for its reception and in fulfilment of this even Jesus had only 12 disciples.

The Secrets of a Master Mason

We may now examine the secrets of a Master Mason against the background of these acceptable norms of society and see whether or not some justification can be found. The science or Royal Art of Masonry is a living and progressive science and our thoughts which must be flexible in their originality must stimulate enquiry which in turn will sustain the Order in these modern times. All that is spiritual is magnetic and the stronger always overcomes the weaker by attraction and/or absorption. 'Unto him that hath more shall be given and unto him that hath not even that which he has shall be taken from him.' Masonry protects the knowledge it has by its secrecy so that it may grow under this Divine Law. Our meeting on the level therefore, while accepting the equality of the Divine spark in every man, anticipates a situation whereby all brethren grow spiritually sufficiently to create an atmosphere of voluntary mutual spiritual interchange based on the law that it is only in giving that we may receive.

Masonry owes its origin and structure to its legendary presence since time immemorial, the growth of the operatives through the Guild system of the medieval ages, and the emergence of the speculatives which is a spiritual outgrowth from application of the principles of the operatives. Masonic secrets must therefore have a base which is legendary, operative or speculative. They are generally termed *The mysterious secrets of a Master Mason* and in their genuine nature are as complex as those of life and revealable only to those who by patience and perseverance prove their title to a participation in them.

The secrets of the operative masons from whence speculative Masonry derives were of a tectonic kind relating to the principles of the art of practical building. They were not academic passwords, Divine names or spiritual privileges. They were technical terms relating to trades that were secretly guarded and seldom communicated to people outside the hereditary groups or clans of Articifers or Guilds.

These mysterious secrets of the operative Master Masons related to geometrical and mechanical principles of construction relating to stresses and strains, to vaulting and ornamentation and similar details of ecclesiastical architecture as this was the golden age of the ministers and cathedrals. It is the refusal to communicate these secrets that resulted in the Hiramic catastrophe that has taken so vital a place in speculative Craft Masonry.

The practice of maintaining secrecy to protect privileged knowledge is no different from the protection of specialized knowledge with the Patents Acts, copyrights or rules of conduct of modern professional organisations. These genuine secrets were substantially lost to the 'Guilds' and 'Companies' with the doctrinal reformation and the dissolution of the monasteries in the 16th century. It follows that even though the secrets also related to mere tokens and passwords of formality and recognition, they also related to principles and the protection of these secrets during the Guild system of operative masons was uniform with all other systems at the time.

In speculative Masonry the mysterious secrets of a Master Mason, while they include tokens and passwords of formality and recognition, relate to the principle of building a moral temple not with hands but ethereal. These principles are now directed towards establishing a way of life based on morality, level steps and square conduct, charity and benevolence, and above all the reverent awareness of the ever pervading Divine influence of the Great Architect of the Universe.

If by its secrecy and silence the Order generates doubts and uncertainties then why do so many people join, knowing that the obligations are taken even before the secrets are revealed? In general, curiosity is not an uncommon sentiment in humanity and to some therefore masonic secrecy generates enough curiosity to motivate them to join. Besides, Masonry developed during the glorious age for the pursuit of secret knowledge — astrology, alchemy, roscrucianism, apocalypse and the Bible in general.

Goronway Owen, an 18th century clergyman, is reputed to have stated that he expected to find in Masonry the hidden mystery of the Druids (J. Moris Jones) ed Llythyrau Goronway Owen 100-1). Dr William Stuckeley, a celebrated 18th century antiquary, states in his autobiography that 'curiosity led him to be initiated into the mysteries of Masonry, suspecting it to be the remains of the mysteries of the ancients'. (*Surtees soc* LXXIII 51).

Secrecy may of course also be a repellent to some minds but in general the greatest attraction and sustaining factor is the ability to perceive intuitively the beauties beyond the secrets as revealed in the lives of the true professors of the Order.

12

MASONRY AND THE BIBLE

The VSL is the spiritual tracing board of the speculative mason; without it he cannot labour and neither can his lodge be properly constituted.

THE RELATIONSHIP BETWEEN the Bible and Freemasonry derives from the fact that Masonry started as an organisation with strong Christian affinities. The Bible was retained in the lodges purely for the obligation of candidates in the same way as state functionaries, witnesses, jurors, etc were sworn.

Masonry ceased to be a Christian organisation at about 1723 with the Andersons *Constitutions* but retained its religiousness thus avoiding the sectarianism of the various Christian organisations. The Bible then evolved into a symbol of masonic faith in the reverent awareness of the existence of God and His will, and the standard of Divine Truth and Justice. This recognition as far as Masonry is concerned was therefore given to any volume that was regarded with the same sacredness and purpose by any group or race. It is for this reason that the Bible or indeed any other sacred book that so qualifies is called in masonic terms VSL (Volume of the Sacred Law).

The important thing is not what book lies open on the pedestal, but it is the book which the Masons who kneel before it venerate as the earthly repository of Divine Truth. Accordingly, for the Jews it is the *Old Testament*, for the Muslims the *Koran*, for the Christians, the *Old* and *New Testaments* of the Bible, for the Brahmans the *Veda* etc.

What is the Bible?

The Bible is the Volume of the Sacred Law, the greater light, pouring forth refulgent rays of Divine Truth from the centre upon the east, west and south. It is regarded by masons as the symbol of the will of God, but perhaps more significantly as the symbol of the unity of God and the reverent awareness of His being, for the sacred writings are to guide our faith and our faith is not in His will but in His Fatherhood which encompasses His will.

It is the rule and guide of our faith, for within its covers are laid down the moral principles and commands for the up-building of our spiritual life. Masonry however seeks for no blind obedience to these commands, and for that reason adherents must be of mature age, and admonished to extend their researches. Freemasonry lays this Book on the altar of faith and it forms the base for the other two great lights, the square and the compasses.

It is the spiritual tracing board of the speculative mason, for without it he cannot labour. It is therefore a landmark of the order that the VSL constitutes an indispensable furniture of every lodge.

It is divine witness to the reality of God, manifesting itself in every living soul with the reassurance that He is found of those who seek Him. It is a volume with unique common appeal, and can now be read in almost every tongue under Heaven. It is the one book that is universally translated, which is a vibrant testimony that God is not far from any tribe, and that His image shines even in the lowest of human beings. It is the one book that has a common appeal and appreciation to the scientist, the poet, the economist, the monarch, the labourer, etc. When the tenets constituting this appeal are translated into the life of humanity, then shall we have the new Heaven and the new earth, where righteousness and peace shall dwell in the manner in which:

> 'Nation with nation, land with land, race with race, colour with colour, unarmed shall live as comrades
> free in every heart and brain shall throb the pulse of one Fraternity
> In vivid expression of the Fatherhood of God and the brotherhood of man.'

'The Bible is said to derive from God to man in general, because the Almighty has been pleased to reveal more of his Divine Will by that Holy Book than by any other means' (Dr Oliver, *English Lectures*).

By the doctrines contained in the Holy Book, we are taught to believe in the wise dispensations of Divine Providence, which belief strengthens our faith and give us hope of becoming partakers of the blessed promises contained therein. It is our duty as freemasons to consider the VSL as a standard of truth and justice and to regulate our actions by the Divine precepts it contains by recognizing the sacred duties we owe to God, to ourselves and to our neighbours.

The Bible is a symbol of truth, Divine Truth, and all truth whether drawn from some book of revelation, some intuitive inspiration, or merely perceiving the great book of Nature. It is not a book of

Fig 11: *The Masonic Pedestal and the Bible.*

philosophy. It does not argue. Indeed, so long ago, St Jerome had described it as 'not a book but a Divine Library'. However men differ in creed or theology, however men differ in culture or upbringing, however men differ in wealth or poverty, however men differ in education or learning, all good men are agreed that within the covers of the Holy Book are found those principles of truth and justice and morality which lay the foundation upon which to build a noble life. There has been no greater testimony to Divine Truth and neither can man vouch for the truth with words more convincing and authoritative than the simple statement 'It is in the Bible' or 'The Koran says so'. These simple statements are pregnant with vitality which surpasses human argument and provides a final proof, for truth.

The Bible is not a record of one mind or even of one age. It is a book of vision whose story starts with Moses and his attempt at moulding men from the chaotic age of Polytheism and sensuality to St John whose inspirational insight is into the final issue of man and his upliftment to the heights from whence he came. Open the Bible and you are suddenly and unconsciously filled with an aura of vastness and vitality, of the presence of some unexplainable force in the drama of humanity in the presence of God, in a story that begins in a garden and forecast inspirationally to the end with the coming of the City of God, against a background of Eternity.

History

As a general practice which is one of the landmarks of Freemasonry, no lodge can be properly constituted for the purposes of any masonic transaction without the VSL lying open on the pedestal, as a symbol of our faith in the Fatherhood of God and His Divine Will.

No one knows for certain when, where and by whom the Bible was brought into Freemasonry, but no mason need to be told the place of honour which the Bible has in Freemasonry. It opens when the Lodge opens and closes when the lodge closes. It is the great light, the symbol of Divine Truth in the Fatherhood of God which Masonry teaches. Indeed, the custom in some American lodges is to present a suitably inscribed Bible from the lodge to the initiate, particularly indicating it as a book peculiarly the cherished chart of the Freemason in his struggle through the storms of life to the harbour of peace. In this struggle there are three duties — to God, to ourselves and to our brethren. It is on record that when George Washington was inaugurated President of the USA in New York on 30 April 1789. Bro Robert Livingstone, Grand Master of New York, administered the oath of office to him, using a Bible from St John's Lodge, and that his first cabinet were all masons except Jefferson. It is also known that almost every name mentioned in the allegories and ceremonies in masonic rituals is biblical, and that scholars have traced from the rituals of the Order up to 75 references to the Bible.

The relationship between Masonry and the Bible is better understood from the history of the development of the Order.

In medieval times Masonry was not only Christian in character, but a Catholic institution. The Guilds, from whence speculative Masonry developed, were religious and toiled in the service of the Church which was almost entirely Catholic, and even had their Patron Saints. Indeed, the oldest document in the Craft, the *Halliwell ms* better known as the Regius Poem, 1390, is catholic in origin and deemed to have been written by a Catholic priest who was a mason, opening with an invocation to the Holy Trinity and the Virgin Mary.

With the Reformation during the reign of Edward VI the Craft became Protestant in its affinities, as shown by the invocation in the old charges of the period such as the *Harleian ms* 1600:

> 'Father of Heaven, with the wisdom of the glorious sonne, through the goodness of the Holy Ghost, three persons in one Godhead bee with our beginning and give us grace.'

The next significant stage of development was the constitution of 1723, otherwise known as the Anderson's *Constitutions*, and particularly the article 'Concerning God and Religion'. This not only severed the craft from Protestantism, but gave it an independent complexion, severing the Craft once and for all from any particular Church, creed, sect, religion or any school of theology.

The ancient charges which are the authentic documents on the law governing Freemasonry contain nothing about the Bible, and there is no evidence prior to 1723 that any significance was given to the Bible except as the Book on which candidates were obligated, precisely as witnesses and jurors were sworn upon in those days. It is presumed therefore that even though the Bible was present in the lodge, it did not assume the symbolic significance it has today. It is on record that in the 14th century the book sacred to some lodges was a copy of the *Old Charges*, which rested on the Master's pedestal. The initiate took his obligations on it. Bibles seem to have been used in those cases after 1725 which took the place of the old charges as the sanction for the candidate's obligation.

In general, it would appear that when and by whom the symbolism of the greater lights was introduced into Freemasonry is unknown. The elevation of the Bible into its present position of eminence was slow. It was accepted as a symbol for the obligations, but it did not become the greater light until about 1760, when on the motion of William Preston in the Grand Lodge of England, it was made one of the great lights. From that day onwards, it has been displayed in lodges in the British Isles and most other countries. As the great light it became and was recognized as the centre, source and symbol of Divine Truth in the Fatherhood of God and His Will which Masonry teaches. Upon the pedestal, supporting the square and compasses, it shines and pours forth refulgent light, a kindly light to lead and a holy law to guide and command. It rules the lodge in all its labour as the Sun rules the day, and masons perambulate in compliance to its path. It became the Volume of the Sacred Law (VSL), it opens when the lodge opens and closes when the lodge closes. No lodge can henceforth be properly constituted for the purposes of transacting any business without the VSL lying open on the pedestal.

Being the great light, to close it would mean to intercept the rays of Divine Light which emanate from it. The Divine founder of the Christian faith had said, 'Neither do men light a candle and put it under a bushel, but on a candle-stick, and it giveth light unto all that are in the house'. Accordingly, the mutual participation in elevating worship by Muslims, Hindus, Chinese, Jews, etc who do not believe in all parts of the Bible is supportive of the Mason's acceptance of the symbolic nature of the VSL.

In Nigeria, lodges in which Christians and Muslims are present keep both the Bible and Koran among the Lodge furniture, both jointly accepted as the VSL, and the initiate is obligated on the volume of his faith. Similarly, in India lodges in which English speaking men sit with Hindus and Mohammedans keep the Bible, the Koran and the Shasters as the VSL in recognition of the symbolic nature of the volume.

The removal of the Book of the law and the substitution of the Book of the constitution by the Grand Orient of France drew considerable protests and withdrawal of recognition and amity from several Grand Lodges around the world. The Grand Orient, however, maintains that by such removal they are conforming with the requirements of the Grand Lodge of England as expounded in 1723 (Anderson's *Constitutions*) 'Concerning God and Religion'. It is also to be recognized that this same constitutional provision led to the controversies inherent in the revival Grand Lodges — The Ancients and The Moderns — that existed for about 50 years before the Union in 1813. Masonry ceased to be the instrument of one particular faith or creed, but rather became the centre for the unification of all creeds by the recognition of their differences. All through these differences and changes, the Bible still occupied its place on the pedestal, shining brighter with greater lustre as the focus of friendship and love and representing one of the greatest attributes of Masonry — faith in the Fatherhood of God.

The controversy was also observable in some lodges in the United States of America at about the same period. In 1820 the Grand Lodge of Ohio resolved that religious tests shall not be a barrier to admission into the first degrees or advancement of applicants, provided they profess a belief in God and his holy word. In 1854, the same body adopted a resolution as follows: 'That Masonry as we have received it from our fathers teaches the Divine authenticity of the Holy Scriptures'. Similarly, in 1845 the Grand Lodge of Illinois declared a belief in the authenticity of the scriptures to be a necessary qualification for initiation.

Although very few masons deny the authenticity of the entire Bible, ie both Old and New Testaments, to require a belief in it as a pre-requisite to initiation will not be in conformity with the express regulations of the Order which demands a belief in God as the only test.

Purpose and Symbolism

Masonry accepts the Bible as a symbol of the presence of our Deity, and just as the foundation of Masonry is based on allegory and symbols, so is the language of the Bible. It has in fact been described as 'a chamber of imagery, a book of parables, a literature of symbols, life depicted in metaphors and similitudes'. Some of them correspond to the symbolism of our working tools and rituals:

> 'Ye also as lively stones are built up a spiritual house.' (I *Peter*, 2-5.)
>
> 'When he set his compass upon the face of the deep, when he marketh out the foundation of the earth.' (*Prov* 5: 27-30.)
>
> 'The Lord stood upon the wall made by a plumb-line with a plumb-line in his hand.' (*Amos* 7: 7-8.)
>
> 'And they went up with winding stairs into the middle chambers.' (I *Kings* VI: 8.)
>
> 'And he reared up the pillars before the temple and called the name of that on the right hand Jachin and the name of that on the left Boaz.' (II *Chronicles* III: 17.)
>
> 'Then said they unto him say now Shibboleth and he said Sibboleth.' (*Judges* XII: 6.)

From these and other passages, it is obvious that the customs, usages, ceremonials and tenets of the masonic Order are so intertwined with the symbolic teachings of the Holy Book that it is neither practical nor prudent for Masonry to exist without a recognition and acknowledgement of the Holy Book.

The Divine purpose of the presence of the VSL in masonic lodges would in my view appear threefold:

1. a symbol of faith in the reverent awareness of the Fatherhood, will and presence of God;
2. a symbol of fidelity in the obligations taken in presence of our Deity;
3. a guide to our faith by the sacred writings contained therein, whereby we are taught the duties we owe to God, to our neighbours and ourselves.

These characteristics which constitute the main purpose of the VSL in lodges are clearly ingrained in the rituals and ceremonials as constant reminders, and if considered in retrospect we find that:

(a) the Master enters the lodge with the VSL borne before him;
(b) the blessing of our Deity is invoked at the opening of each degree, and the lodge declared opened in the name of God, at which time the VSL is opened by the appropriate officer;
(c) the blessing of God is again involved at the closing of each degree, and the lodge is closed in the name of our Deity, at which time the VSL is closed by the appropriate officer;
(d) every candidate for initiation and advancement pledges that he hopes to obtain the privileges by the help of God and he is allowed to enter the lodge in the name of the GAOTU etc;
(e) every candidate for Initiation declares his belief and trust in God in all cases of difficulties and dangers, that his faith may be well founded;
(f) every candidate in every degree takes and seals his obligation in the presence of and on the VSL, accepting the sacred writings as the guide to his faith;
(g) we are charged to consider the VSL as a standard of truth and justice, and to regulate our activities by the Divine precepts it contains, as therein we find the duties we owe to God, to our neighbours and ourselves;
(h) the attention of every candidate is deemed to be particularly arrested by the Hebrew characters in the middle chamber now depicted in FC Lodges by the letter G which refers to the GAOTU to whom we must all submit, and whom we ought most humbly to adore;
(i) we are reminded of the sacred symbol which alludes to the GAOTU in the centre of the building, the blazing star, the glory in the centre.

Finally, we find all these lead to the discovery of the centre, the point within the circle from which a mason cannot err. The point is said to be bounded by the two grand parallels north and south representing Moses and King Solomon, or the two Patron Saints St John the Baptist and St John the Evangelist. On the upper part of the centre rests the VSL which supports Jacob's ladder.

Were we as conversant with the Holy Book, and as adherent to the doctrines therein as those two grand parallels were, it would bring us to Him who will not deceive us, nor suffer deception from us. In traversing this centre, we must touch both these parallels as well as the VSL, and while a mason keeps himself thus circumscribed he cannot possibly err.

Bible Opening

If we accept the symbolism of the VSL in all respects in relation to masonic ceremonies, the holy Book should not be opened at random. In each degree can be found an appropriate passage in the Holy Book that relates to the design and significance of all or part of that degree, and in a properly conducted lodge the opening of the VSL should bear some relevance to the design of the degree worked. Unfortunately masonic usage has not always been constant, nor is there a universal agreement as to what passage should be opened in each degree. It is said that in an intelligently conducted lodge the VSL should be opened at the first chapter of St John, the Patron Saint of Freemasonry 'if perchance the words will meet the candidate's eye, to make him realise that the basis of his being is the Divine word shining within his own darkness'.

In the 1° *Psalm* 133 appears to be appropriate:

'Behold how good and how pleasant it is for brethren to dwell together in unity'.

In the 2° I *Kings* 6:8 appears to be appropriate:

'an allusion to the winding staircase in the middle chamber'.

or

Judges 12, in allusion to the symbolism of the password of the 2° SHIBOLETH at the conflict between Jeptha and the Ephraimites.

In the 3° *Ecclesiastes* 12 would appear appropriate:

'Remember now thy Creator in the days of thy youth' in allusion to the ceremony of the Hiramic Legend.

The custom in America at least since the publication of Webb's *Monitor* has been fairly uniform, as follows:

In the 1° it is *Psalm* CXXXIII, an eloquent allusion to and description of brotherly love.

In the 2° it is *Amos* VII 7:8, an allusion to the plumb-line, an important emblem of that degree.

In the 3° it is *Ecclesiastes* XII 1-7, a description of old age and death appropriately applied to the sacred object of this degree.

It is however true that at different periods various passages have been selected but always with great appropriateness. It is appropriate that a judicious study be made of the Holy Book and the DC be allowed the option of opening the book at any of the appropriate passages.

Still in the USA, the following passages have also been applied at certain times:

In the 1°, *Gen* 22, an account of Abraham's intended sacrifice of Isaac;

or

Gen 28, a record of the vision of Jacob's ladder;

In the 2°, I *Kings* 6:8, an allusion to the door and winding staircase to the middle chamber;

or

II *Chronicles* III 7, an allusion to the two great pillars, Boaz and Jachin.

In conclusion, it may be stated that, to the mason it is not only the appropriateness of the passage that lies open that matters, but the book combined with the square and compasses representing faith, hope and charity, and at the same time wisdom, truth and justice, the qualities that emanate from the Great Architect of the Universe, all of which tend to keep our lives circumscribed within the centre from whence a mason cannot err.

13

THE HIRAMIC LEGEND

Ancient spiritual, religious and mystery Orders have a common base in the communication of Divine truth through the medium of legends which may be mythical, historical or philosophical, and to this extent Masonry also excels.

MASONIC KNOWLEDGE IS communicated principally in three modes namely legends, allegories and symbols, all designed as vessels for the communication of eternal truth. While symbols are designed to be material representations of truth, legends on the other hand are mental and philosophical representations of truth, and it is the emphasis on the mental communication of truth that masonic legends are out to teach.

It is an incontrovertible fact that the entire fabric of masonic philosophy is built around a single legend — THE HIRAMIC LEGEND — a legend which is partly historical, partly factual, and partly symbolic, dealing with the building of a temple in Jerusalem by Solomon, King of Israel. This legend now generally so constitutes a very important part of the masonic ritual, and consequently by constant repetition even the symbolic part may seem to have been converted into a myth which over the years has assumed the status of a truthful narrative to the extent that even some masons of higher titular rank are often unable to distinguish the myth from its symbolic import.

The central legend is the building of an unfinished temple, and commences with King Solomon's desire to build a temple to the glory of Jehovah, and his difficulty in finding skilful workmen and artisans to superintend and execute the architectural part of the designs. The Tyrians and Sadonians were at the time known to be celebrated artists and mechanics throughout the then known world, and Tyre was indeed one of the principal seats of the Dianysiac Fraternity of Artificers, a society engaged exclusively in the construction of edifices, and operating under an organization probably subsequently imitated by operative masons.

The King of Tyre Hiram was a friend and allay of King Solomon and King Solomon made an appeal to his ally for the pleasure of the use of his most able builders and artisans. Hiram King of Tyre granted this request by dispatching vast numbers and quantities of men and material to King Solomon. Among the men was a distinguished artist who was in possession of all the skills and knowledge to carry out the plans and designs of King Solomon. This celebrated artist was Hiram Abif who was in all probability a member of the Dianysiac Fraternity of Artificers, and who was given the superintendence of all the men, and whom masons call sometimes 'the Builder', sometimes 'Our Master' and at other times 'the Widow's Son' whose fidelity in the sacred trusts reposed in him, was strong enough to make him prefer death than improperly disclose the secrets of a Master Mason. The narrative further states that Hiram was responsible for the preparation of the plans and designs, and that the temple was virtually finished within the short space of seven years and six months to the amazement of all the world, but the celebration of the capestone by the fraternity with great joy was interrupted by the sudden death of the Master Builder Hiram Abif. The narrative continues that the conspiracy was originated by 15 fellows of craft of that superior class appointed to preside over the rest, and who finding that the temple was nearly completed, and that they were not yet in possession of the secrets of a master mason, decided to obtain them even by recourse to violence. The conspiracy resulted in the eventual death of the Master Builder Hiram Abif; the loss of the plans and designs and the associated secrets, and a general and utter confusion among the craftsmen. The subsequent details as to the search for the body and interment are matters that need not be gone into in this volume but suffice it to say that by the sudden death of the Master Builder the secrets of a master mason were lost.

An account of this narrative is found in I *Kings* VII 13, 14, in a passage that reads as follows:

> 'And King Solomon sent and fetched Hiram out of Tyre. He was a widow's son of the tribe of Naphtali, and his father was a man of Tyre, a worker in brass, and he was filled with wisdom and understanding, and cunning to work all works in brass. And he came to King Solomon and wrought all his works.'

The second book of *Chronicles* II (13, 14) bears testimony of the granting of King Solomon's request by Hiram King of Tyre, and refers to Hiram the celebrated artist in the following manner:

'And now I have sent a cunning man endued with understanding of Hiram my father's; The son of a woman of the daughter of Dan, and his father was a man of Tyre, skillful to work in gold and in silver, in brass, in iron, in stone and in timber, in purple, in blue, and in fine linen, and in crimson; also to grave any manner of graving, and find out every device which shall be put to him with my cunning men, and with the cunning of the Lord David thy Father.'

Accordingly it is observed that the narrative is amply recorded in the scriptures, but nowhere in the scriptures did the narrative extend to the level of a legend. The narrative in the Holy writ states that the Temple was completed, it was destroyed, rebuilt and destroyed again on more than one occasion. Furthermore, the Holy writ made no reference to the conspiracy, or even to the death of the Master Builder. On the other hand, the scriptural narrative states that the building was completed by Hiram in every particular, and consequently, from history and facts, no temple built of stones and with hands would appear to have remained unfinished through the death of a professional architect such as Hiram is supposed to have been in the 'Hiramic Legend' which is the base rock of masonic philosophy. The legend further states that by the death of the Master Builder, the genuine secrets of a Master Mason are lost, and masons are merely now in possession of substituted secrets, and will continue the search until time and circumstance will restore the genuine. The narrative in the Holy writ does not appear to support this. The particular plans and designs may have been lost, but the principles of architecture, the genuine secrets of the building trade have never been lost, even though skills and design may have deteriorated, and changed in response to altered socio-economic circumstances. Indeed, many temples built after the temple at Jerusalem surpass that temple in size and magnificence, and it would be absurd on the surface to imagine that masons are waiting for time or circumstance to restore the genuine.

In the scriptures, *Abif* refers to that celebrated builder sent by Hiram King of Tyre to superintend the building of the temple at Jerusalem by King Solomon. In some context, the word means 'his father' as witness the reference made in *Chronicles* IV 16, as King Solomon's father. In some other context, such as the *Vulgate*, English translations, Luther, the Swedish translator, the word is regarded as an appellative or surname. In Hebrew on the other hand, the word is often used as a title of respect, and may therefore signify counsellor, wiseman or anything else equivalent just as Eghon in Yoruba, Imor in Ogbia, Etc in Calabar, and Dianyi in Igbo. It could even mean benefactor, master, teacher etc or Oga in Pidgin. Freemasons regard it as well as a title of respect and distinction bestowed on the widow's son, the Chief Builder of the temple. The word also meant Chief, Duke or Head, and these titles were generally used as surnames in those days.

The legend would appear to have been passed down by oral narrative through the ages, but it has been preserved without alteration in its mythical form. When it originated, by whom and where is largely unknown, and when a degree was made out of it is also unknown.

The 'old charges' do not contain the tragedy, nor is it contained in any other records prior to 1725-30. It would however appear to be an enactment of a central fact in the daily life experiences of the Masonic Guilds portraying the strains and stresses inherent in the organisation of a vast number of artisans in one common bond, under strict regulations and codes of conduct. The earliest written form of this legend is found in Andersons *Constitutions* 1738. Therein, the temple is said to have been finished in a short space of seven years and six months to the amazement of all the world; when the capestone was celebrated by the Fraternity with great joy. But their joy was interrupted by the sudden death of their dear master Hiram Abif, whom they decently interred in the lodge near the temple according to ancient usage.

In the next edition of the same constitution published in 1756, a few additional circumstances were included relating to the participation of King Solomon in the general grief, and the ordering of his obsequies to be performed with great solemnity and decency by King Solomon.

It is significant to observe here that the factual content of the narrative relates that Hiram Abif arrived Jerusalem in 1012, for the purposes of the building of the temple at Jerusalem but Freemasonry as a speculative fraternity is said to be a little over 250 years old. May it therefore not be that masonic philosophy refers to the building of a temple different from the historical temple at Jerusalem by King Solomon? May it not be that masonic philosophy invites us to pierce the veil of this legend to understand its real import by contemplation?

The real import of the legend would appear to relate to the desire of all ancient mystery orders and rites to teach as their cardinal object the doctrine of the immortality of the soul through death and subsequent regeneration. Traces of this belief and the doctrine are found even in the most primitive of pagan societies and philosophies through the ages, even though the form of presentation may vary according to the rites performed. The temple in respect of which Hiram was the Chief Architect relates symbolically to 'building in eternity', a temple not made with hands, eternal in the heavens, a spiritual temple embodied in both the spirit and organism of man, man's life structure. In the overriding concept of the immortality of the soul, history, legend, philosophy, and myth appear to have been inextricably mixed over the years, and yet producing a common ground.

Following from this we find that the story of the building of the temple is a philosophical instruction in a garbled historical form leading to a revelation of the structure of the human soul, and its relationship with the human organism. The Jerusalem referred in the legend could not be the Jerusalem geographically located in Palestine or Israel, but the 'Jerusalem on High' — the 'Grand Lodge Above'. The stones are the 'unhewn stones' of the human spirit with which it was the grand design of the Creator to establish humanity in perfectness.

Accordingly the legend contains some elements of discrepancies and lack of logic which lend support to the view that 'it is a rite' and not a drama. It has no plot and it is not strictly history. From the point of view of time scale, Freemasonry as a fraternity which is not more than 250 years old could not have had its original base philosophy from a physical temple built several years back. The opening and closing ceremonies of the third degree reveal the whole philosophy — the legend is designed to inculcate — the entry of the human soul from the east, the sojourn to the west which is the world of matter, the experiences gained from a development of our intellectual skills, and search for the lost secrets and the journey back home but with only substituted secrets which will designate us all until time and circumstance shall restore the genuine.

It is the desire to understand this basic philosophy that the different legends of physical death are meant to teach. The death referred to is not physical death but a spiritual experience which we have to pass through, transfiguring everything when we become aware. When by constant endeavour and contemplation, the body, the encasement of the soul vibrates in harmonious resonance with the spirit in such a way that all actions of the body are the direct responses of the spirit impulse rather than sensual reflexes, then the stage of death unto life has been achieved, and the desires of the body die in order that the desires of the soul might live. It is only this condition that allows the spirit at physical death to soar with such lightness to the luminous heights from whence it came, the Grand Lodge above. To live therefore means dying.

Masonry teaches these lessons through the acquisition of the basic disciplines of virtue morality and brotherly love, a constant adherence to the cardinal virtues of prudence, temperance, fortitude and justice, just in the same way as the student who practices law, architecture, engineering, surveying, accountancy is taught the basic disciplines of the particular profession as a guide.

The Holy writ states in *Psalm* 23:

> Even though I pass through the valley of the shadow of death, I shall fear no evil, for Thy rod and Thy staff shall comfort me, and I shall dwell in the house of the Lord for ever.

The temple referred in the Hiramic Legend is 'collective humanity' for St Paul even said in his inspiration 'know ye not that ye are the temple of God?' It was the intended desire of the Creator to establish humanity with perfect souls who would be privileged to share in Divine knowledge and truth. Masonic legend states that the secrets of this Divine knowledge were known to only three in the world. Conspiracy and blatant desire for the extortion of the secrets of a higher degree had caused the fall of man, and the loss of the secrets just the same way as stated in the allegory of Adam and Eve in the garden of Eden. It is only time and circumstance that would restore the genuine with our own endeavour and the instructions of the Master.

The calamity that befell the craftsmen is the unfinished human nature, and we know not how to complete it, just as was stated in the scriptures 'They have taken away my Lord, and I know not where they have laid Him', humanity having been deprived of supreme wisdom by its mysterious disappearance is left with the substitutes of intellect and sensuality. We as craftsmen are in search of the body which represents the lost supreme wisdom and consciousness. In this search we in humanity go our different ways according to our beliefs, some hoping to find it in science, some in religion, some in Christianity or even paganism, others in sensuality each confirming the fact that we are conscious of the loss, and yet many of us make no discoveries whatsoever all through the journey. Those who search farthest and deepest in great earnest with hope, faith and charity are those who become conscious of the serious significance of the loss, and who are therefore compelled by share volition to exclaim 'Machabone', 'Macbenah' just as was exclaimed by Mary in the Holy Scriptures 'They have taken away the body of my Lord'.

We are however consoled by the glimmering ray of our five senses and rational faculties, and the promise that even in this perishable frame resides a vital and immortal principle which still inspires a holy confidence that we will be enabled by the Lord of life to sustain the hope for peace and consolation in the discovery of our lost spiritual wisdom.

Hiram is said to personify the lost Divine wisdom. Hiram according to the legend was by the order of King Solomon interred in a befitting sepulchre near the Holy of Holies. We are said to represent that sepulchre, and deep down in us is that immortal principle, that

Divine spark which resides even in this perishable frame of ours, never losing its lustre.

The sepulchre is said to be outside the Holy City 3ft between North and South, 3ft between East and West, and 5ft or more perpendicular. This is said to refer indeed to the human body with the sepulchre in the centre of our system. Just as the 'Divine Will' is the centre of creation — the Universe — controlling and giving life to it, and the Sun is the centre of the solar system giving life, energy and motion to the planets around it, so the spirit or the Divine spark is the centre of man giving life and energy to man in support of the Biblical assertion:

'The Kingdom of Heaven is within you . . .'

We are told that we hope to find the lost secrets with the centre, and the centre is described as a point within a circle from which all parts of the circumference are equidistant, and that it is a point from which a master mason cannot err. It is commonplace knowledge that points, circles, and circumferences have no relationship with the science of practical building, and therefore the legend as performed in the 3° expresses in clear terms the universal truth that mystical death precedes mystical birth. The Scriptures confirm this in the following manner:

> Know ye not that ye must be born again . . .
>
> Unless a grain of corn fall into the ground and die, it abideth alone, if it die, it bringeth forth much fruit . . .

The ceremonial drama of this legend re-emphasises this philosophy by asserting in the following manner:

> It is thus my brother, that all Master Masons are raised from a figurative death to a higher life and a fuller knowledge of the teachings of our mysteries — 3° *Rituals*.

The Hiramic legend therefore reveals the process of invocation of the spirit essence in the natural man to a consciousness of the entire homogeneous species around him, by the death of his entire sensuality.

'The fall of man', 'the lost word', 'the death of our Master', 'the original sin' or by whatever other name it may be called is a philosophic concept unanimously recorded as being a fact from the wisdom tradition of the sages in antiquity, and from all scriptures of all races through the ages, no matter how far removed one race from the other in time or distance, and no matter how simple or elaborate the system. They are all a pointer to the root doctrine of all religions — the origin and destiny of the soul of man. From this point of view, the legend may be analysed and taken in parts:

(a) The acquired skills of the master Builder in terms of knowledge and cunning.
(b) The conspiracy of the Fellows of Craft.
(c) The sudden death of the Master Builder and the utter confusion that ensued.
(d) The disappearance of the body and the subsequent search.
(e) The re-interment of the body with all ceremonies and respect.
(f) The raising of the body — birth into new life.

These are held to epitomise the Hiramic legend as the symbol of human nature in its development in the life here and the life to come.

His skills are a symbol of his moral stance, his intellectual capacity, his temperance, his fortitude, his prudence, his justice and all other social and moral virtues, which, with the assistance of the sacred writings in the volume of the Sacred Law, he lays down carefully on the Tracing Board of his life for the building of his moral temple.

The conspiracy is a symbol of the wordly temptations and tribulations of sensuality, disease, worldly possessions, etc which debase the body and cause its vibrations to lower its harmonious resonance with the spirit.

He may overcome these by the standard of virtue he possesses, but will finally succumb to his inevitable destiny which is physical death, when the silver cord is broken, and the soul departs from its encasement thus throwing darkness and utter confusion to the material world. The gross material search is usually in vain for what should be found is ethereal and not material.

The raising of the body symbolizes the transportation of the human spirit to the Grand Lodge above from whence it came, after its interment as near as possible to the *Sanctum Sanctorum* which is primordial or even Divine where no human spirit can dwell because of its density, and inability to withstand the intensity of Divine light pressure.

The restoration of the human spirit from the collective fall of humanity as represented by the Hiramic legend and biblically by the Adamic legend is described to be an act that is developed through the paths of heavenly science.

> We are guided by the principles of moral truth to contemplate the spiritual or hidden mysteries and trace their developments along the paths of heavenly science or royal art.

It is this science of the spiritual rebuilding of the human race that is common in all religions in all races, lands, and ages. It is the eternal law 'as it was in the beginning, is now, and ever shall be, world without end'. For the purposes of this regeneration God has never left Himself without a witness among the children of men, and among the witnesses of this ancient wisdom is Masonry.

In the expression of this inherent human desire, history is replete with examples and similarities through the ages. A parallel is easily drawn even in the four gospels in the trials, death, burial, disappearance and search for the body, and the resurrection of the son of God.

In similar manner, the myth of Adonis in the Syrian mysteries, while differing in its details and construction with the Hiramic legend in Masonry, coincides in its object which is the teaching of the doctrine of restoration to eternal life from death.

In Egyptian mythology, Osiris representing the sun was assailed and slain. Darkness ruled for a moment, Isis went on search, Osiris was later resurrected and brought to life. The same was true of Mithras in the Persian mysteries, of Dionysius in the Grecian and Syrian mysteries and of Bacchus in the early Roman rites. All were slain, sought for, and finally raised and brought to life. All portray the belief in immortality which has been in the human mind in his spiritual philosophies from remotest antiquity.

This belief is also symbolised in very strong terms in ancient African rites such as *OBHINORU* at birth and *OPURU ODIOLI* at death, each symbolising a belief not only in the immortality of the soul, but also that physical life begins with the introduction of the soul, and ends with the departure of the soul.

OBHINORU is an ancient rite practised among the ancient communities of Ogbia in Southern Nigeria. It symbolizes both the immortality and regeneration of the soul and an extension of the doctrine of re-incarnation. Its basic belief is that the birth of a new child takes place only by the re-entry or regeneration and sponsorship of the soul of a departed relative whose life pattern influences to a large degree the life pattern of the new child. Accordingly the new child is usually named after the departed relation, and by a process of continuation common names develop along definite family lines, for the re-entry and sponsorship can only be within the extended family unit.

OPURU ODIOLI practiced by the same communities symbolizes both the immortality of the soul and the end of physical life at the departure of the soul. Its basic belief is that at physical death, the living soul must publicly account of its deeds on earth before it is transported to the ethereal. This public account is a solemn rite whereby the soul is invoked to express symbolically how virtuous or otherwise it has lived its life while on earth, for a soul that has lived without virtue does not qualify to sponsor the birth of a new child.

It is also in acknowledgement of this belief in the immortality of the soul that libations of drinks are symbolically poured and offered to departed ancestors in several ancient spiritual and mystery rites.

In similar manner analogies of the legend can be drawn from the Sabian worship of the sun and the heavenly bodies celebrating the death and resurrection of the sun. The solar orb was adored at its resurrection in the morning from its apparent death of the evening, the rising being considered as an emblem of the regeneration of the soul.

Other vivid analogies are found in the Mosaic myth of Adam and Eve, and the forbidden apple, the cosmic parable of the prodigal son, and the myth of Demeter and her daughter Persephone.

According to this myth, Persephone strayed away from Arcadia to pluck flowers in the meads of Enna. The soil opened underneath her, and she fell into the lower world of Hades, ruled over by Pluto. Demeter's despair reached Zeus, the Chief of the Gods, who decreed that if Persephone had not eaten of the fruit of Hades, she should be restored to her mother for ever, but if she had so eaten, then she must abide a third of the year with Pluto. She had eaten of the fruit.

From all indications, myths had been regarded from time immemorial by all mystery and religious orders as an important and convenient vessel for instruction, purification and enlargement of human imagination, understanding, and awareness of Divine truth as expressed in the origin, destiny and the immortality of the soul and the process of its regeneration through death. It is an affirmation of the established creative will of God, that there can be no life without death. Greek mythologist were particularly adept in expressing cosmic and philosophical truths in fables which reveal theosophic knowledge to the discerning and perceptively conscious while at the same time veiling these from the ignorant and indolent. To that extent therefore myth making was not an indulgence in irresponsible fiction, but an inspired science. It is for the reason that the true meaning is usually veiled that differences in interpretation are prevalent even though the cardinal theme of the legend remains mythically the same.

The problem of understanding the masonic system is therefore the problem of understanding our inner self, relying on the consoling promise that by our own endeavour and the instructions of the master, time and circumstance will restore the genuine, as we are now only in possession of the substituted secrets of our being.

Let us therefore remember that in whatever form the Hiramic legend is dramatised in our ceremonial, it is merely a symbolic narrative that is designed to instruct us in the understanding of the mythical teachings and knowledge of our whole being.

Plate I: *The author when Right Worshipful Master.*